Extraordinary Results
From Ordinary Teachers

by Michael D. Warden

Group

Loveland, Colorado

Extraordinary Results From Ordinary Teachers

Credits
Author: Michael D. Warden
Editors: Bob Buller and Dave Thornton
Creative Development Editor: Paul Woods
Chief Creative Officer: Joani Schultz
Copy Editor: Pamela Shoup
Designer and Art Director: Kari K. Monson
Cover Art Director: Jeff A. Storm
Computer Graphic Artist: Joyce Douglas
Cover Desiger: Lighthouse Communications Group
Production Manager: Gingar Kunkel

Library of Congress Cataloging-in-Publication Data
Warden, Michael D.
     Extraordinary results from ordinary teachers / by Michael D.
Warden.
          p.   cm.
     Includes bibliographical references.
     ISBN 0-7644-2013-5
     1. Christian education--Teaching methods. 2. Jesus Christ-
-Teaching methods. I. Title.
BV1534.W34   1998
268' .6--dc21   98-13489
                                                                 CIP

10 9 8 7 6 5 4 3 2 1   07 06 05 04 03 02 01 00 99 98
Printed in the United States of America.

Contents

Introduction 4

Chapter 1: **You Can Teach as Jesus Taught!**......................9

Chapter 2: **Jesus the Rabbi?** 25

Chapter 3: **Why Jesus Taught** 42

Chapter 4: **Using Sayings and Parables** 69

Chapter 5: **Discourses, Discussions, and Debates**............91

Chapter 6: **Learning Through Experience**.....................114

Chapter 7: **Asking the Right Questions** 136

Chapter 8: **Showing the Way**...157

Chapter 9: **Your Game Plan for Teaching Like Jesus** 177

Scripture Index 201

96183

Introduction

Teaching in His Steps

"I walk in the Way
Sojourner is my name
for I am a traveler
through lands I only pretend to know...
But I do pretend."[1]

L et me tell you a story.

When I was younger, say, eleven or so, I discovered writing for the first time. A little-known aunt of mine had given me a journal for my birthday, and told me I had to fill it up with dreams and stories and poems and pictures and anything else that delighted or distracted my heart. I was enthralled. The creative muses in me awakened as I flipped past blank page after blank page, wondering at the possibilities of what I might create to fill them.

From that time, I set out in earnest to write. I kept notes from my daily experiences, wrote songs (all blissfully simplistic, as I recall), composed letters to God—even drew pictures to illustrate my many fanciful stories. That journal became my doorway to secret realities; my own personal "wardrobe to Narnia."

But then school happened. Or more specifically, *junior high* school. It took only a few months to realize that I had this writing thing all wrong. There were rules to follow, set down by books and stern-faced elders. I plodded through the spelling tests and sentence diagrams (blech!), but still held to what I felt was real about writing—all the places it could take you and all the ways it could change you.

But eventually my schooling began to take its toll. Slowly, painfully, my writing began to change. People didn't care much about what I said, I realized, so long as I said it well. *That* was what brought the A's and the accolades. In time I became an expert pretender at writing—focusing on form and totally denying the need for impact. And I fooled everyone with my oh-so-pithy style.

Until I met one especially irritating man.

His name was Mr. Warren (I never knew his first name), and during my senior year in high school, he was my Honors English professor. He was a crusty, middle-aged chain smoker who had a raspy old laugh and a biting flair for sarcasm. And, as it turned out, a great sense of what was real about writing.

After turning in my first essay to him, he turned it back with no grade. There were no spelling corrections; no red marks reworking my grammar. Just two words written in huge red letters at the top of the first page:

"SO WHAT?!"

I went up after class and asked for a grade. He said it didn't deserve one. I asked him why. He said the essay didn't say anything. I asked him what he thought of the writing style. He said it didn't matter. The content wasn't real.

With just a few gruff words, that man blew my cover. Exposed me for what I was. I was a pretender at writing, and he knew it. He called me on it, laid it out plainly before me, then nailed it to the page.

So What?

In 1 Corinthians 2:10, Paul tells us that "the Spirit searches all things." As Christian education directors, Sunday school teachers, small-group leaders, mentors, and parents, that means the Spirit of Christ sifts through every word we speak (or fail to speak), every question we ask (or fail to ask), and every gesture or choice we make before those we presume to teach. And he carefully examines the fruit of our labors, borne out in our lives, and, we hope, in the lives of our students.

He searches the depths of your life that way—and mine. So I have to ask: If he came to me today, having looked at everything about my teaching that there is to see, and asked, "So what?"

What would I tell him?

What would you?

I'll tell you what I have said at times. I've told God that it's impossible to expect me to teach like Jesus. After all, Jesus was perfect, and I am not. He had miraculous power at his disposal to drive his point home, and I do not. He had a perfect grasp of Scripture, and I do not. He could see people's hearts clearly, and I do not. He absolutely understood the mind of God, and I...I find God more mysterious now than when I first met him.

And yet, we're *commanded* to live like Jesus. First John 2:6 tells us quite clearly that "whoever claims to live in him must walk as Jesus did." And right in the middle of his famous Sermon on the Mount, Jesus set out the standard by which we all must measure our lives. "Be perfect, therefore, as your heavenly Father is perfect" (Matthew 5:48).

How ironic. I mean, why would God command me to do something that's so obviously beyond my grasp as a Christian? Does that sound like God to you? Me neither.

In his classic devotional *My Utmost for His Highest,* Oswald Chambers writes:

> If Jesus ever gave us a command He could not enable us to fulfil, He would be a liar; and if we make our inability a barrier to obedience, it means we are telling God there is something He has not taken into account. Every element of self-reliance must be slain by the power of God. Complete weakness and dependence will always be the occasion for the Spirit of God to manifest His power.[2]

Perhaps the problem is not in the command, but in my ability to take it seriously. Perhaps I don't believe in God's power in the way I think I do. Perhaps my arrogance is too large and my God is too small.

I believe that most of us who stand in front of Christian classrooms today are pretenders, just as I was in Mr. Warren's class. We say we believe in the power of Christ's Gospel, but then habitually place our trust instead in rote tradition. We stay far on the safe side of teaching, using traditional techniques such as passive lectures, fill-in-the-blank work sheets, puzzles, inane discussion questions, and token prayers. Perhaps we have secretly learned that people don't care much what we say, so long as we say it in the way they want us to.

I've taught in churches for over fifteen years. I've taught children and preached to the elderly. I've tried to be sincere and faithful to the truth, even when I've been exhausted, wounded, angry, or confused. I've done my best with what I know, as we all have.

But imagine just for a moment that there was something more. What if you learned that there was a whole new level of teaching that goes far beyond anything you'd ever experienced, perhaps even beyond anything you'd ever seen firsthand? What if you learned that this new form of teaching could not only revolutionize your students' learning and their lives, but it would definitely revolutionize your life as well? Would you be interested in learning more about it? Would you be willing to risk trying it?

The Journey Begins

In the following chapters, we'll embark on an exploration of Jesus as a teacher, and strive to discover how we can translate Christ's teaching style and his methodology into our own teaching in the church. We'll dismantle many arguments people have used over the years to say that teaching like Jesus is impossible. And we'll compile a list of principles that we can apply right away to our teaching—principles that Jesus himself relied on and used to help people learn.

But I won't be guiding us through this journey alone. Much of what is contained in these pages is the result of many weeks of intensive group study by a handful of creative and educational leaders at Group Publishing, Inc. These leaders include:

Thom Schultz—CEO of Group Publishing, Inc.

Joani Schultz—Chief Creative Officer

Joel Fay—Product Division Vice President

Bill Korte—Product Development Department Leader

Paul Woods—Creative Development Editor

Rick Lawrence—Editor of GROUP Magazine

Christine Yount—Editor of Children's Ministry Magazine

And me, Michael Warden—Former Creative Development Editor

All of us together searched the Scriptures and our own experiences for an answer to the question this book addresses: What does it mean to teach the way Jesus taught? We came away from this study with some startling answers and a few lingering questions. In the pages that follow, we want to share all of our discoveries with you and challenge you in the same way we were challenged—to start a revolution in Christian education, based on the way Jesus taught.

In the end, my hope is that we'll all be transformed from ordinary to extraordinary teachers. I also hope that we will be transformed as disciples of Jesus. He is, after all, the point of our teaching.

"He is before all things, and in him all things hold together."

—*Colossians 1:17*

---

[1] Michael D. Warden, *Sojourner.*
[2] Oswald Chambers, *My Utmost for His Highest* (Uhrichsville, OH: Barbour and Company, Inc., 1992), 91.

Chapter 1
You Can Teach as Jesus Taught!

"Then Jesus came to them and said,
'All authority in heaven and on earth
has been given to me. Therefore go and make disciples
of all nations, baptizing them in the name of the Father
and of the Son and of the Holy Spirit,
and teaching them to obey everything I have commanded you.
And surely I am with you always,
to the very end of the age.' "
—*Matthew 28:18-20*

Jesus was a master teacher. On that one point, you'll find little debate—from just about anyone. People may not believe Jesus was God or that he died and rose from the grave, but they'll still grant that Jesus was one of the greatest teachers in history. And of course, we agree. As Christians, we believe there could be no better teacher than Jesus. His teaching defines what teaching is all about.

So why don't we teach the way he taught?

Doesn't it seem ironic that we as Christian educators stand in front of our students each week and tell them to "be like Jesus" in the way they live, and all the while we aren't willing to "be like Jesus" in the way we teach? Talk about mixed messages!

And yet the arguments against teaching like Jesus continue to dissuade us from trying. There's only one thing wrong with all of these arguments: They're wrong! You can teach the way Jesus taught. In fact, you should!

Let's take a look at some of the more prominent arguments we typically hear:

1. Jesus was God. He possessed supernatural insight that helped

him in his teaching. We can never measure up to that.

Yes, Jesus was God. His knowledge was vast, his wisdom flawless. He knew the Scriptures perfectly, and could see clearly into the hearts of the people he encountered. And these are all qualities none of us possess within ourselves.

Perhaps we're overlooking a very important truth. It isn't quite accurate to say only that Jesus "was" God. Jesus *is* God. He rose from the dead! He lives forever now, never to die again. And where does he live? In you!

"I have been crucified with Christ and I no longer live, *but Christ lives in me.* The life I live in the body, I live by faith in the Son of God, who loved me and gave himself for me" (Galatians 2:20, author emphasis).

"I pray that out of his glorious riches he may strengthen you with power through his Spirit in your inner being, so *that Christ may dwell in your hearts through faith*" (Ephesians 3:16-17a, author emphasis).

"I have become [the church's] servant by the commission God gave me to present to you the word of God in its fullness—the mystery that has been kept hidden for ages and generations, but is now disclosed to the saints...*which is Christ in you, the hope of glory*" (Colossians 1:25-26, 27b, author emphasis).

Jesus was God, and he still is. He still has supernatural insight. He still knows just the right words to say or the best thing to do in every teachable moment we encounter. And because Jesus, the *master teacher,* lives within us, we can teach the way Jesus taught—by letting him teach through us!

The Bible puts it this way:

"For God, who said, 'Let light shine out of darkness,' made his light shine in our hearts to give us the light of the knowledge of the glory of God in the face of Christ. But we have this treasure in jars of clay to show that this all-surpassing power is from God and not from us" (2 Corinthians 4:6-7).

And,

"Whoever claims to live in him must walk as Jesus did" (1 John 2:6).

It isn't arrogant or ludicrous to believe that we can teach as Jesus taught even though he is God. It's a command!

2. I don't even understand God myself. So how can I expect to be able to teach as Jesus taught?

Do you think the original twelve disciples understood Jesus? They were people just like you and me (maybe even a little more rough around the edges than you or me). And though they followed him, they did not fully understand him. Very often, Jesus would say things, do things, or tell them to do things they didn't understand, but they followed him anyway, and God blessed them. (For some examples of confused but obedient disciples, take a look at Mark 4:35-41; Luke 9:10-17; or John 13:1-9, to name a few.)

Another passage, Mark 6:7-13, briefly describes the time Jesus sent out the twelve on a sort of short-term missionary journey. Jesus knew they didn't yet fully understand him or his purpose, but he sent them anyway. And they obeyed.

And do you know what happened when his disciples obeyed? Scripture says, "They went out and preached that people should repent. They drove out many demons and anointed many sick people with oil and healed them" (Mark 6:12-13). Apparently obedience pays off, even when we don't fully understand the reason behind God's command.

Of course, understanding is important in our relationship with God. We all want and need to come to a complete "knowledge of the truth" (1 Timothy 2:4). But if we choose to wait until we fully understand everything about God before we'll step out to follow him, we'll never do anything. And we'll miss the powerful purpose he has for our lives today.

3. Jesus used teaching methods that were effective for Jewish culture in his time, but they would never work today.

Granted, Jesus lived in a time and place quite different from our own. For example:

- He had no permanent classroom.
- He didn't use a set curriculum.
- He didn't follow a set schedule.
- There was no formal grading or reward system.
- He never gave a written assignment.
- He never gave a written exam.
- He often taught "on the go" from one place to another.

And, of course, cultural differences affected the way Jesus taught. He used the common items and events of his day as examples of spiritual truths. He spoke of sheep, wineskins, sowing and reaping—not the sorts of things most of us encounter on a daily basis anymore.

But does that mean we can't translate his teaching methods into our modern culture? Of course not! Christian educator Roy B. Zuck writes:

> How he [Jesus] gained interest, how he stimulated thinking, involved students, told stories, applied truths, answered questions, dealt with individuals of varying personalities and differing attitudes toward him, motivated and corrected students—these are a few of the many areas where we can learn from his style.[1]

Another educator, Lois E. LeBar, writes:

> Students of Scripture sometimes wonder how our teaching today can be compared with Christ's teaching when He never taught in a classroom and we seldom teach outside one. What difference do four walls make? Often they make the teaching atmosphere formal and mechanical, but not necessarily so. A teacher who realizes that only individuals can change and grow will act as informal and make as much use of personal conversation as Christ did.[2]

Once they're translated into modern culture, Jesus' teaching methods work as well today as they did when he used them two thousand years ago. The human mind and heart have not changed in all that time. And neither has the way we learn best—Jesus' way.

4. To teach as Jesus taught, I'd have to spend years studying his teaching style and adopting it as my own. I just don't have that kind of time.

Not so! Jesus' teaching methods, for the most part, are clear, direct, and easy to duplicate. And the best part is they work! All that's required of you is the willingness to approach education the way Jesus did and risk trying it for yourself!

In addition, when it comes to teaching as Jesus taught, you have a few distinct advantages already inside you, planted there by God himself. First, because you're a Christian, the Holy Spirit lives inside you and will help teach you how to teach like Jesus. Consider these encouraging words:

"But the Counselor, the Holy Spirit, whom the Father will send in my name, will teach you all things and will remind you of everything I have said to you" (John 14:26).

"But when he, the Spirit of truth, comes, he will guide you into all truth" (John 16:13a).

"We have not received the spirit of the world but the Spirit who is from God, that we may understand what God has freely given us. This is what we speak, not in words taught us by human wisdom but in words taught by the Spirit, expressing spiritual truths in spiritual words" (1 Corinthians 2:12-13).

Those are some pretty powerful confidence-builders, aren't they! And that's not all! Because Jesus lives in you, you have access to an incredible resource for teaching! Here it is:

" 'For who has known the mind of the Lord that he may instruct him?' But *we have the mind of Christ*" (1 Corinthians 2:16, author emphasis).

What a powerful resource! In addition, we also have spiritual gifts at our disposal to help us teach like Jesus. So even though learning the "nuts and bolts" of Jesus' teaching style is important, you don't have to be a Bible scholar to do it. All you have to be is willing.

But be warned! Although teaching like Jesus is simple, that doesn't mean it will be easy. It will require you to take risks in ways that may make you (and your students) uncomfortable. It may even require you to do some things that some people might consider offensive.

But that doesn't sound very Christian, you say? Oh, yes it does. Read on. You'll see what I mean.

Risky Love

Some years ago, I was working as a youth pastor at a small country church down in Texas. My good friend Don was also a youth pastor in the area, and just about every Christmas his youth group would corral lots of local teenagers to go caroling through small-town neighborhoods on a flatbed "hayride" trailer. It was always loads of fun and a great opportunity for new kids to join the group.

One particular Christmas, Don was especially interested in reaching out to one young man named Jeremy. Jeremy was a spunky junior high kid who seemed to be on a collision course with self-destruction. His parents had been seriously struggling in their relationship for years, and it seemed a break up was imminent. Their problems had taken a heavy toll on Jeremy, and in his confusion and anger he blamed God for his pain, then left the church to join a less wholesome crowd. Don continued to reach out to him, with limited success, for a few months. But then another blow came on Jeremy's heart. His dog—and best friend in the world—died suddenly. From then on Jeremy shut out all contact with Don, the church, and with God.

So on this particular Christmas, after several months of long silence, Don called Jeremy and invited him to the caroling hayride. To everyone's surprise, Jeremy said yes. With cautious excitement, Don told me about Jeremy's plans to attend, and Don and I immediately prayed together that Jeremy would, in fact, come and that this evening would prove to be the start of a new healing for his wounded heart.

As the night for the event approached, Don came down with a painful stomach virus. Concerned that he would not be able to attend his own event, he asked me and a few other youth leaders in the area to come to the hayride as additional (and possibly, replacement) leaders for the kids.

I showed up at the event that night and ran directly into Jeremy. He looked sullen, hesitant, and suspicious. But he was there. And I was thankful. Don made it as far as the church that night, then collapsed on a couch, too nauseous to stand. The other youth leaders and I herded the kids onto the trailer, and off we went, caroling through the neighborhoods of that small Texas town.

About midway through our trip, something terrible happened. (I still get a knot in my stomach just thinking about it.) A couple of kids started roughhousing in the front of the trailer. One of them, a beautiful young girl, caught her foot under the wheel guard, and was pulled from the hay where she sat. Her body was caught by the movement of the tire, and it pulled her under the trailer, right into the path of the wheels.

Within moments, the trailer dragged to a halt. Laughter became screams. And a young girl lost her life. That beautiful girl's name was Katie. And the young boy who had been roughhousing with her was Jeremy.

He ran from the scene, and we never found him again that night. A few days later, Don called to talk with him, but he was not willing. We all prayed all the more fiercely for Jeremy, but from all the evidence we could see, this tragedy had dealt a fatal blow to Jeremy's faith.

Of course, we knew God didn't cause any of this to happen, but still I wondered how God could have allowed it to occur. A young Christian girl—lost. Her family horribly bereaved at Christmastime. And a young man who was now probably convinced that God must hate him to allow so much pain to come to his young heart.

Nobody heard from Jeremy for months. He didn't attend church and didn't talk to anyone much. It was a small town, after all. Everyone knew what had happened. And although it was an accident, Jeremy acted like the town leper, weighted with the impossible guilt of Katie's death.

But then, sometime after spring break, news began to trickle in to the church from kids in Don's youth group. Jeremy was talking to people. But he wasn't talking about sports, school, or the weather. He was talking to them about Jesus.

It seems that Jeremy got a copy of his school's student directory. And every day after school, he would ride his bike from address to address, talking to his schoolmates about what had happened to him and Katie and about God's mercy and forgiveness. He wanted all of his schoolmates to know God's salvation.

What happened to Jeremy revolutionized his life. He knows God's mercy now in a way few of us can match. But the tragedy could have prompted him to shut out God forever. It was all dependent upon the condition of Jeremy's heart and upon his willingness to run *to* God and not away from him.

God is profoundly risky in how he loves us. He's willing to risk losing us to gain us. He's willing to let us be hurt on the chance that we might let him heal us. He's willing to let us wrestle with confusion and disillusionment, in the hope that we will seek him diligently and with humility until we finally "come to a knowledge of the truth" (1 Timothy 2:4b). This "reckless" love characterizes and encompasses everything that God does.

Now I'm going to make a connection that may seem radical to some of you. It certainly will seem radical (and maybe even ludicrous) to many church boards out there. But it is key to understanding what it means to teach as Jesus taught. OK, ready? Here it is…

God can be profoundly risky in how he *teaches* us.

Notice I didn't say that God is always risky in how he teaches. He isn't. Oftentimes his instruction is gentle, patient, and long-suffering. We all know that from Scripture and from personal experience. But Jesus isn't always a Lamb when it comes to teaching. Sometimes he is a Lion. He can be willing to risk losing us over an important lesson in the hope that we'll choose to be teachable, humble, and receptive to seeing things from his perspective. One mentor of mine often says that when it comes to walking with Jesus, "If you can be offended, you will be offended." In other words, the instruction of Christ has a way of sifting through our attitudes and beliefs to challenge any pretension we have "that sets itself up against the knowledge of God, and...take captive every thought to make it obedient to Christ" (2 Corinthians 10:5).

That sifting has a way of ticking us off because at the core it tends to challenge our perceptions of who Jesus is. And who we aren't.

The Holy Spirit teaches us in exactly the same way Jesus did. The Spirit uses parables, experiences, words of insight, and Scripture—all with the same effect Jesus' teaching had while he lived on earth. Some of us will reject the Truth. Others will be indifferent (or blind) to it. But some—not the majority—will be drawn toward God in a way that radically transforms them for all eternity.

Risky Teaching

We are called to teach as Jesus did. Christ has come to live inside us; we've been given the Holy Spirit to help us accomplish this task. It's what Jesus' Great Commission is all about:

"Then Jesus came to them and said, 'All authority in heaven and on earth has been given to me. Therefore go and *make disciples* of all nations, baptizing them in the name of the Father and of the Son and of the Holy Spirit, and *teaching* them to obey everything I have commanded you. And surely I am with you always, to the very end of the age' " (Matthew 28:18-20, author emphasis).

Here's the challenge: As Savior, Lord, and Teacher, Jesus had no problem alienating some people in his efforts to develop committed followers. Understanding that principle is crucial to understanding not only how Jesus taught, but how radically different our teaching will become as we follow him.

Consider, for example, the discourse between Jesus and a crowd of Jews who followed him across the Sea of Galilee to Capernaum after the feeding of the five thousand. The teaching is found in John 6:44-59. As you read this account, put yourself in Jesus' place *as a teacher.*

"No one can come to me unless the Father who sent me draws him, and I will raise him up at the last day. It is written in the Prophets: 'They will all be taught by God.' Everyone who listens to the Father and learns from him comes to me. No one has seen the Father except the one who is from God; only he has seen the Father. I tell you the truth, he who believes has everlasting life. I am the bread of life. Your forefathers ate the manna in the desert, yet they died. But here is the bread that comes down from heaven, which a man may eat and not die. I am the living bread that came down from heaven. If anyone eats of this bread, he will live forever. This bread is my flesh, which I will give for the life of the world."

Then the Jews began to argue sharply among themselves, "How can this man give us his flesh to eat?"

Jesus said to them, "I tell you the truth, unless you eat the flesh of the Son of Man and drink his blood, you have no life in you. Whoever eats my flesh and drinks my blood has eternal life, and I will raise him up at the last day. For my flesh is real food and my blood is real drink. Whoever eats my flesh and drinks my blood remains in me, and I in him. Just as the living Father sent me and I live because of the Father, so the one who feeds on me will live because of me. This is the bread that came down from heaven. Your forefathers ate manna and died, but he who feeds on this bread will live forever." He said this while teaching in the synagogue in Capernaum.

Not exactly a great way to win people over, is it? Eat my body, drink my blood, and you will have eternal life. Of course, from our perspective two thousand years after the event, we understand that Jesus was talking about spiritual food—he even says so in the latter part of the passage. But for the majority of the crowd that heard him, his teaching could have sounded like cultic cannibalism and the drinking of blood.

In The IVP Bible Background Commentary, Craig Keener writes:

Jewish people had many forbidden foods, but all the Greco-Roman world abhorred cannibalism (which some abominable cults and some barbarians reportedly practiced occasionally)...On the literal level (cannibalism and drinking blood) obeying Jesus' statement should have merited judgment, not salvation; thus they are confused.[3]

In addition, according to Jewish law in Leviticus 17:10-11, drinking the blood of any creature was always forbidden. So, yes, they were definitely confused! Jesus no doubt knew the law, and no doubt understood how easily his teaching would be misinterpreted by the crowd. Surely he could have thought of a way to explain the same truth without alienating so many of his listeners. So why didn't he? Why did he choose to express his teaching in such an offensive way? What was he thinking?

Luckily we don't have to guess what Jesus was thinking, because he explains his actions right there in the passage. If we just jump back a few verses before his "blood and flesh" teaching, we can hear Christ explain one of the cornerstones of his philosophy of learning. Here it is:

"If [Jesus] had spoken plainly, [his listeners] wouldn't have to put forth any effort to understand what he was saying. You hear it and it's out of your mind already. But if he does or says something in a way that initially doesn't make sense, he creates this distance that you have to pursue, that you wouldn't otherwise."

—Rick Lawrence

"No one can come to me unless the Father who sent me draws him, and I will raise him up at the last day. It is written in the Prophets: 'They will all be taught by God.' Everyone who listens to the Father and learns from him comes to me" (John 6:44-45).

And to re-emphasize the point, he says again in verse 65, "no one can come to me unless the Father has enabled him."

What does Jesus mean? Without getting into controversial discussions about foreknowledge or predestination, I think we can safely make the following statement, which is one of many principles of teaching like Jesus that we'll highlight throughout the book.

Principle 1
Realize that people cannot understand truth unless God enables them.

In other words, trying to teach children, youth, or adults about God or his ways is useless unless God is working in their lives through the Holy Spirit. This principle may seem obvious at first glance, but its implications for teaching are profound. For example, without understanding this principle, we may end up spending the majority of our energy and time trying to teach students whose hearts aren't really teachable or open to God. Instead, we should focus our attention on those whom God is drawing in (see John 6:44-45). (More on how to discern between the teachable and the nonteachable in a moment.)

In addition to focusing our energy in the wrong place, if we don't grasp this principle, we'll also be far less likely to try anything risky in our teaching for fear of offending some of our students or fellow leaders. But if Principle 1 is right, then some people *should* be offended by our teaching. Consider Paul's instructions in 1 Corinthians 2:14, "The man without the Spirit does not accept the things that come from the Spirit of God, for they are foolishness to him, and he cannot understand them, because they are spiritually discerned."

> *"I think in education so often we're just comfortable. We think, 'I don't want anybody to be uncomfortable.' And Jesus never was afraid of making people uncomfortable."*
>
> —Joani Schultz

The truth is by its nature foolish to those who don't accept it. That means our teaching should be offensive to some people, at least some of the time. If it isn't, we have to wonder whether we're actually teaching God's truth at all.

Now before you go running off to offend someone in the name of God's truth, we have to ask a very important question:

How can you tell a teachable heart from a nonteachable one?

Unfortunately, even in the most extreme cases, this distinction isn't obvious. For example, I've actually had the opportunity to share my faith with a few Satan worshipers. I was on a summer missionary trip in south Texas. Right in the middle of one of our group's outdoor meetings, two Satanists walked up behind me, gas can in hand, looking for a ride to the nearest gas station. Seems their jeep had run out of gas, and they were stranded on the nearby road. They had no idea the gathering they stumbled upon was a Christian missionary meeting, but once they realized it, they identified themselves as Satan worshipers and began cursing us and our God. One of the pair had a knife strapped to his right shin and even boasted about his skill in using it to "get revenge on all you weak Christians." A friend of mine and I led the pair away from the crowd so we wouldn't disturb the meeting, and we talked with them for over an hour about Jesus and our faith. After a time they both calmed down, so much so that we agreed to take them to get gas (a decision that seems foolish to me now, but at the time seemed the right thing to do). However, despite repeatedly presenting the message of Christianity to these two fellows, we felt like we were getting nowhere. I remember thinking that trying to teach these guys about Jesus was like trying to teach a brick to fly.

So can I say definitively that their hearts were not teachable? Absolutely not! To this day, I don't believe talking to them was a waste of time. Perhaps in time our words would sink in. I'm simply not in a position to tell. Only God knows.

As I said, this is an extreme example. In more typical classroom situations, there's even less of a potential distinction between those who are open to God and those who aren't. The student whose eyes are wide and attentive may have a heart as cold as stone, while the student who seems the most distracted (or distracting) may be the one who truly learns.

But there *is* a way to distinguish between those who are teachable and those who aren't. Jesus used this "secret" method all the time as a way of assessing the "learning potential" of any group of people he dealt with. Rather than trying to guess who to focus his energy on, Jesus actually used his own teaching methods as a tool for sifting the crowds, separating out those people whose hearts weren't really spiritually hungry from those who were open to God's truth. That's why Jesus sometimes used experiences, examples, stories, or metaphors that could easily seem offensive or even confusing to people—to confront their pride, to make them think, and, if their hearts were teachable, to provoke them to dig deeper for an explanation.

> *"Making people think goes further in changing their hearts than simply giving them a rule to obey."*
> —Paul Woods

Notice that's exactly what happens in John 6:60-69. After hearing Jesus' difficult teaching on eating his flesh and drinking his blood, many of his disciples questioned Jesus' instruction. Jesus responded by saying, "Does this offend you? What if you see the Son of Man ascend to where he was before! The Spirit gives life; the flesh counts for nothing. The words I have spoken to you are spirit and they are life" (John 6:61b-63). And although the Scripture says that from that time on many of his disciples left him, when Jesus asked the Twelve whether they were going to leave also, Peter responded by saying, "'Lord, to whom shall we go? You have the words of eternal life. We believe and know that you are the Holy One of God'" (John 6:68-69).

> *"Rather than...setting out with the mind-set, 'I'm going to exclude some,' I set out with the mind-set, 'I'm going to teach the only way people can learn, and some will exclude themselves.' "*
>
> —Rick Lawrence

Clearly, there was a powerful difference between the hearts of many of Christ's would-be disciples and Peter's heart. And that difference was exposed through the way Jesus taught.

Jesus the Risk Taker

It's clear from the previous story that Jesus, as a teacher, was a risk taker. There is a plethora of other examples of Jesus' "risky" teaching. In the chapters that follow, we'll explore each of his methods in detail, but here's a quick overview of some of the ways Jesus took risks in teaching:

• **Through parables.** A parable is simply a truth wrapped in a story. Jesus probably used parables because he understood that people quickly forget facts and figures, but they'll remember stories. Parables are risky, though, because they can be easily misinterpreted or misapplied. You can never predict what a person might glean from a story. You can never be certain that he or she will get the point you intend.

Jesus faced this problem all the time. His disciples often didn't understand his parables. Certainly a large portion of the crowds who heard him teach in parables walked away perplexed, never grasping the real truths Jesus was illustrating. And yet, Jesus didn't explain his parables unless he was asked. And he never chased after people who listened to make sure they understood what he meant. What would happen if you took that risk in your classroom? What would your students say? How would other people react?

• **Through discourses, debates, and discussions.** Just read a few of the things Jesus said in his lectures, debates, and discussions:

"You nullify the word of God for the sake of your tradition. You hypocrites!" (Matthew 15:6b-7a).

"If your hand or your foot causes you to sin, cut it off and throw it away" (Matthew 18:8a).

"Is it not written: 'My house will be called a house of prayer for all nations'? But you have made it a 'den of robbers' " (Mark 11:17).

"I tell you the truth, anyone who will not receive the kingdom of God like a little child will never enter it" (Luke 18:17).

"You belong to your father, the devil, and you want to carry out your father's desire" (John 8:44).

And that's just a sampling! Jesus said many shocking, provoking, and offensive things when he spoke in front of crowds or discussed issues with smaller groups. He did not avoid controversy, but rather used controversy to provoke his hearers to think and learn—or to leave. There is no provision in Jesus' words for indifference.

Is that how you teach?

• **Through experiences.** If your brother was dying, and you sent word to Jesus to come quickly to heal him, but Jesus didn't come, and your brother died—how would you respond? Jesus did that with Lazarus, Mary, and Martha in John 11. If you were with a friend on a boat, when suddenly Jesus appeared to you walking on the water, and your friend stepped out in faith and walked on the water toward him—how would you feel? Jesus did that with his disciples in Matthew 14:22-33. If Jesus miraculously appeared to all of your friends, but not to you—what would you do? Jesus did that with Thomas in John 20:19-29.

Jesus even sent out his disciples to practice what he was teaching them. He didn't try to go along with them. He wasn't available for the questions that inevitably came up. And he didn't try to control the situations they encountered. He just sent them and trusted the Holy Spirit. Talk about risk! What if they failed? What if they did something to embarrass Christ? What if they weren't ready for what they would face?

Jesus took risks with people—even those closest to him. He orchestrated experiences that forced people to grapple with uncomfortable thoughts and emotions. He did not insulate his disciples from disillusion, defeat, rejection, fear, pain, or betrayal. Neither did he hold them back from joy, laughter, peace, healing, power, or love. He allowed it all and even welcomed it, because he knew that true faith must confront gritty reality to be proven as real. Do you allow those kinds of experiences in your class?

● **Through questions.** Has anyone ever asked you a question that effectively ripped through your pretense and exposed your heart for all the world to see? If you know what that's like, then you know that the way you reacted to the question revealed more about you than the answer to the question ever could.

Jesus used those kind of "soul-exposing questions" often. Most times he never expected a spoken answer. There was no need. The faces of his listeners said it all. The questions he asked provoked more than a simple answer—they provoked change.

Using questions like that was risky for Jesus. He made a lot of people angry. Some of them got so angry that they decided to kill him. But for some people, Jesus' questions helped provoke them to go out and change the world. Do your questions do that?

● **Through modeling.** Jesus was not your typical rabbi. Although he walked in purity before God, he held little regard for the religious traditions of his day. He laughed with sinners, shared meals with tax collectors, and even allowed a woman to publicly wash his feet with her hair. He publicly denounced the religious leaders of his day. Yet he touched lepers, played with children, and spoke to Samaritans.

There was a message in Jesus' life—one that wasn't conveyed in words, but in actions. At times, his actions seemed so extreme that his family thought he was insane (Mark 3:20-35). And yet the life he modeled established a pattern his disciples would later follow as they took his message all over the world.

What sort of pattern are you modeling for your students?

What About Now?

So what about teaching like Jesus in the here and now? Should we just walk into our classrooms tomorrow and start spouting off truth in risky, offensive ways? I mean, Jesus did it. He made it work, so why can't we, right? Well, yes and no. You see, it's one thing to examine Christ's risky style of teaching in Scripture and call it "good," but it's also important to carefully examine what it would take to effectively transfer his teaching methods into a modern Christian classroom or mentoring relationship. For this reason, as we attempt to apply Jesus' teaching methods to a modern context, there are several important "filters" we will consider. For example,

- the influence of Jewish culture on Jesus' teaching style,
- the differences between ancient Jewish culture and our modern western culture,
- the particular audience Jesus dealt with each time he taught,
- the goal(s) of Jesus' teaching, and
- the fact that Jesus is the Son of God and not an ordinary person.

By taking Jesus' teaching experiences through these filters, we will discover many powerful ways we can transfer Jesus' teaching style and methods into a typical classroom setting or mentoring relationship. The results of applying these discoveries in your classroom or relationship should be extraordinary, if not revolutionary!

And maybe, if you're teachable, God will revolutionize your life in the process.

[1]Roy B. Zuck, *Teaching as Jesus Taught* (Grand Rapids, MI: Baker Books, 1995), 13.
[2]Lois E. LeBar, *Education That Is Christian* (Tappan, NJ: Revell Publishing, 1958), 50. Quoted in *Teaching as Jesus Taught*.
[3]Craig S. Keener, *The IVP Bible Background Commentary: New Testament* (Downers Grove, IL: InterVarsity Press, 1993), 280.

Chapter 2
Jesus the Rabbi?

"The crowds were amazed at his teaching,
because he taught as one who had authority,
and not as their teachers of the law."
—Matthew 7:28b-29

Rabbis just aren't what they used to be.

I don't mean that disrespectfully. I just mean they aren't. Well, not exactly.

Webster's defines a rabbi as "an ordained spiritual leader of a Jewish congregation." To become an ordained rabbi, a man must attend a Yeshiva, which is a rabbinical school typically attached to a particular synagogue. Once ordained, rabbis usually act within their synagogues as the modern equivalent of Protestant pastors or Catholic priests. They teach, counsel, and comfort their members in much the same way spiritual leaders of other faiths do.

But this is not the way it has always been. In fact, the definition of what it means to be a "rabbi" has shifted several times over the centuries. Originally, the title (which means "my great one") was used to address any person in a respected position.[1] Not too long before Jesus' time, the title came to be used almost exclusively in reference to esteemed teachers (although it was also occasionally used by a slave in reference to his master or by an apprentice when referring to a craftsman in a particular field)[2]. During this time, the title connoted a personal connection (thus the translation as *"my* great one"). Later, the word lost its possessive quality and came to refer in general to authorized teachers of Jewish law. Finally, the word developed into its modern usage, as a specific title for Jewish men who have been through special training to become ordained as rabbis.[3]

I tell you all this to ask a question: Was Jesus actually a rabbi?

In order to really answer the question, and then apply it to our modern-day role as teachers, we have to set up one important ground rule. We have to assume that any exploration of Jesus as a rabbi must be taken in the context of what "rabbi" meant in his day, not in ours. Many modern rabbis may be offended at the suggestion that Jesus was a rabbi at all, perhaps because they measure him against modern standards for the title, rather than standards more appropriate for the time he lived on earth.

Teacher's Corner: Teacher or Rabbi?

According to the New International Dictionary of New Testament Theology, the Greek word *didaskalos* (translated as "teacher") typically referred to people who "regularly engaged in the systematic imparting of knowledge or technical skills: the elementary teacher, the tutor, the philosopher, also the chorus-master who has to conduct rehearsals of poetry for a public performance."[4]

Rabbi, on the other hand, was a reverential form of address, typically used "as the title of the authorized teachers of the Law."[5]

In fact, even though Jewish leaders today often don't accept Jesus as a rabbi, the religious leaders of Jesus' day had no problem addressing him as such. Jesus was called rabbi or teacher more often than any title other than "Jesus," "Lord," or "Son of Man."[6] (For a more detailed breakdown of the ways people addressed Jesus, see "Titles for Jesus" below.)

Titles for Jesus[7]

Title	Occurrences in Matthew	Occurrences in Mark	Occurrences in Luke	Occurrences in John	Total
Jesus	170	97	97	251	615
Lord	47	11	53	40	151
Son of Man	29	15	26	10	80
Teacher or Rabbi	15	17	22	16	70

We've already noted that the meaning of "rabbi" in Jesus' day typically carried a personal connotation. Jesus wasn't just a "great one;" he was "my great one." That may be why Jesus' disciples called him "rabbi" more than anyone else. Likewise, that may explain why Jesus' opponents never used the title "rabbi" with him, typically opting for the less personal title *didaskalos,* which was the Greek word for "teacher." This fact will become important later, when we explore the different ways Jesus chose to teach these two groups.

So was Jesus recognized and regarded as a respected teacher by most of the people he encountered? Absolutely. But he was unlike any rabbi who had ever come before him or any who would follow after.

Not Your Typical Rabbi

Wherever Jesus went, he stirred up controversy. He questioned norms. He openly rejected the status quo and challenged people to look at life from a new perspective. Understandably, the religious teachers of his day weren't sure what to do with him. In their eyes, he was a young, upstart rabbi, who had never been formally trained, and who seemed bent on dismantling the religious structure they had committed their lives to uphold.

You see, even though today's system for becoming a rabbi is more precise than it was in Jesus' day, there were still certain commonly recognized steps for anyone who wanted to become a teacher of the law. There were rabbinical schools, even then, in either the synagogue or the priests' homes. Almost all rabbis were trained as disciples of older, more experienced rabbis—individuals whose teachings they typically followed to the letter. In fact, this saying is commonly attributed to rabbis: "Nor have I ever in my life said a thing which I did not hear from my teachers."[8]

"The people had come to see God and his kingdom through the Old Testament. Jesus came to bring a new understanding and new revelation of who God was and what his kingdom was about, and so he constantly dealt with the old perception and almost attacked it by showing what his kingdom was really like."

—Rick Lawrence

Jesus did not follow the traditional route to become a teacher. The truth is we don't really know much about the route he did take. All we know is that when he began to teach, "the crowds were amazed at his teaching, because he taught as one who had authority, and *not as their teachers of the law*" (Matthew 7:28-29, author emphasis). It's not hard to get the idea that Jesus was pretty unconventional in his approach to teaching. He ignored the accepted routes for "respected" teachers and relied instead on the authority of God to get his point across.

It's important to understand that Jesus *chose* this unconventional route to becoming a rabbi. He could have submitted to the religious systems of his day. He may have even gained credibility (in the eyes of the religious leaders, anyway) if he had trained under older teachers as other rabbis did. But he didn't. And there's a reason—one that we should heed as teachers today.

In John 7:14-24, Jesus reveals his reason. It was on an occasion when Jesus came to teach in Jerusalem during the Feast of Tabernacles. Once Jesus began to teach, the Scripture says:

"The Jews were amazed and asked, 'How did this man get such learning without having studied?' Jesus answered, 'My teaching is not my own. It comes from him who sent me. If anyone chooses to do God's will, he will find out whether my teaching comes from God or whether I speak on my own. He who speaks on his own does so to gain honor for himself, but he who works for the honor of the one who sent him is a man of truth; there is nothing false about him' " (John 7:15-18).

"This whole passage from the Sermon on the Mount, where he's talking about, 'You've heard it said,' so much of that is talking about the external rules they followed. 'You've heard that it was said, "Don't murder. Anyone who murders is subject to judgment." I say, "Anyone who is angry with his brother is subject to judgment." ' To me, Jesus is trying to get people to focus on the heart and not on rules."

—Paul Woods

In Jesus' day, rabbis relied on the authority of other rabbis to support their teaching. Jesus never did this. In fact, he countered many of the accepted teachings of his day by offering a radically different teaching of his own—"But *I* tell you..." (Matthew 5:22, 28, 32, 34, 39, and 44).

It was as if the Jewish teachers were asking, "Who taught you to teach these things? You have never studied under any of our respected leaders. You've never even mentioned another rabbi by name. Where are you getting this teaching that you proclaim with such authority?"

And Jesus' answer could have been, "My teaching and my authority are based on God's truth and do not rest on the faulty, fickle opinions of human teachers."

The Apostle Paul (who was, by the way, formally trained as a Jewish teacher of the law) lays out that argument again for us in his letter to the Corinthians. In 1 Corinthians 1:26–2:5, he writes:

"Brothers, think of what you were when you were called. Not many of you were wise by human standards; not many were influential; not many were of noble birth. But God chose the foolish things of the world to shame the wise; God chose the weak things of the world to shame the strong. He chose the lowly things of this world and the despised things—and the things that are not—to nullify the things that are, so that no one may boast before him. It is because of him that you are in Christ Jesus, who has become for us wisdom from God—that is, our righteousness, holiness and redemption. Therefore, as it is written: 'Let him who boasts boast in the Lord.' "

Then Paul drives the point home in the verses that follow:

"When I came to you, brothers, I did not come with eloquence or superior wisdom as I proclaimed to you the testimony about God. For I resolved to know nothing while I was with you except Jesus Christ and him crucified. I came to you in weakness and fear, and with much trembling. My message and my preaching were not with wise and persuasive words, but with a demonstration of the Spirit's power, *so that your faith might not rest on men's wisdom, but on God's power."* (author emphasis)

In the same way, our teaching must not be based on human wisdom. Instead we must learn to let God work through us as we teach so that his power and authority are revealed.

Now, please don't misunderstand. This doesn't mean we should exile all of our theologians, silence the great Bible teachers of our day, and burn down our seminaries. Christian education is good and important. We should all be students of the Bible and learn as much as we can from the wisdom of other Christians who have gone before us. But when it comes to effectively teaching the way Jesus taught, a seminary degree will in no way guarantee your success. But once we've done our studies and prepared our lessons to the best of our abilities, the authority and the ultimate effectiveness of our teaching must rest on God alone.

That's good news! It's a great relief to know that God doesn't demand that we all get doctorate degrees before we'll be effective teachers for Christ. All he demands is that we stay true to the Bible and that we rely completely on his Spirit to impact others through us.

Basing teaching on God's authority instead of human wisdom was only one of the ways Jesus "the rabbi" differed from his contemporaries. Here are a few others. As you read them, think about how they might apply to you as a teacher today.

Rabbis...*taught people to follow religious traditions that went beyond the demands of Scripture.*

Jesus...*rejected religious traditions that resulted in hypocrisy.*

One of the classic examples of this controversial difference between Jesus and the Pharisees is recorded in Mark 7:1-13. During this time, Jesus is in Jerusalem with his disciples, and many of the "Pharisees and some of the teachers of the law" gathered around to keep an eye on him (Mark 7:1). The passage describes how the Pharisees saw some of Jesus' disciples "eating food with hands that were 'unclean,' that is, unwashed. (The Pharisees and all the Jews do not eat unless they give their hands a ceremonial washing, holding to the tradition of the elders. When they come from the marketplace they do not eat unless they wash. And they observe many other traditions, such as the washing of cups, pitchers and kettles)" (Mark 7:2-4).

To understand the significance of what Jesus' disciples were doing, we need to understand a bit about the Pharisees' beliefs.

The name "Pharisee" means "the separated ones." They believed that one reason the nation of Israel had suffered in exile was because it broke God's law (which is the truth of the matter, by the way). Consequently, the Pharisees committed themselves to obeying God's law in every detail and promoted the same kind of absolute obedience among all the Jewish people.[9]

In *The New Manners and Customs of Bible Times*, Ralph Gower explains that the Pharisees "wanted to be legally pure, separate from any form of defilement. They believed that the difference between being 'clean' and 'unclean' depended upon that law. What was 'clean' was obedience to the law; what was 'unclean' was disobedience to the law."[10]

But there was just one problem. Even though Moses handed down 613 laws for Israel to obey, some of the commands were too vague to know exactly how to apply them to everyday situations. For example, what exactly did it mean to keep the Sabbath day "holy"?

So to help people avoid breaking God's law, the Pharisees promoted an exhaustive set of guidelines that took the Law of Moses and applied it to almost every contemporary situation people might encounter. These guidelines were created and revised over several generations, until they had become the respected "tradition of the elders" that the Pharisees mention in the passage in Mark.

The issue isn't that far removed from modern Christianity. The New Testament is also vague about several issues Christians face. For example, is it always a sin to chew tobacco, smoke, or drink alcoholic beverages? The Bible doesn't offer a definitive command one way or the other. But many Christian leaders do, most often because they're genuinely concerned about keeping people from falling away from God or stumbling into self-destructive behaviors.

So maybe we can understand why the Pharisees questioned Jesus about his disciples' behavior. After all, if Jesus' disciples weren't concerned about staying ritually clean, couldn't that be a "first step" toward disregarding the rest of the law as well?

But instead of commending the Pharisees for their concern about obeying God, this "upstart" Rabbi lashes out at them. He says,

"Isaiah was right when he prophesied about you hypocrites; as it is written: 'These people honor me with their lips, but their hearts are far from me. They worship me in vain; their teachings are but rules taught by men.' You have let go of the commands of God and are holding on to the traditions of men" (Mark 7:6-8).

"Any time you expose something, some of the people around you are going to be furious at being exposed."

—Rick Lawrence

Why would Jesus respond so forcefully to the Pharisees' question? After all, what if you were the person Jesus was talking to, only you had asked the question after seeing one of his disciples pop open a can of beer?

The issue we're addressing here isn't whether drinking is right or wrong, any more than it was whether it was right or wrong for the

> *"I think Jesus was trying to get them to think outside of the normal confines of life, outside of the physical, the temporal. I think they had, as I think we have in a lot of ways, gotten caught up in following rules and doing the daily actions, and not seeing beyond to think in terms of eternity or the kingdom. He was trying to get them to think, as we would say, 'out of the box.' "*
>
> —Paul Woods

disciples to eat without first ceremonially washing their hands. The issue, then and now, is whether or not we have a right attitude toward God's Word. The Word of God is *not* incomplete. It is not right for us to add to Scripture whenever it seems vague, any more than it would be right to remove Scriptures that we don't feel comfortable with. As a teacher, Jesus understood that the Word of God must not be tampered with. And even though they may have had good intentions, that's exactly what the Pharisees had done.

Gower adds, "The crux of the matter seems to have been that in seeking to live according to the law, the Pharisees had failed to understand what the law was all about."[11]

It's not hard to understand why the Pharisees made this mistake. And it's not hard to see how we could make the same mistake as teachers, especially when our personal convictions are so strong that we promote them as biblical truth, even when they aren't.

Rabbis...relied primarily on repetition so their students would remember their teachings verbatim.

Jesus...relied upon experiences and other teaching methods to help his disciples remember the essence of his teaching.

Rote memorization is a time-honored practice among educators, dating back to the days of the Pharisees and before. We can picture it easily: a robed rabbi, seated in the temple courts with students all around, leaning in, listening to them repeat his teaching.

"A generous man will prosper; he who refreshes others will himself be refreshed," says the rabbi. Then, pointing to one of his students, he says, "Now, you."

The student responds, "A generous man will prosper; he who

refreshes others will be refreshed himself."

"No," says the rabbi. "Listen. A generous man will prosper; he who refreshes others will himself be refreshed. You must listen. Now, again." The student clears his throat then starts again, "A generous man..."

Now switch the scene to modern times. Let's place ourselves in a Sunday school classroom, with a teacher sitting on a chair, and a dozen or so children gathered around her on the floor.

"OK, kids, listen now," says the teacher. "Listen so you can say it after me, OK? Here we go.

"A generous man will prosper; he who refreshes others will himself be refreshed" (Proverbs 11:25).

"OK, now you try."

The children squirm as they join their voices in a jumble of mumbles. "A generous man will man prosper refreshes..."

The teacher interrupts, "OK, listen closely now. And this time, let's try it in smaller chunks...A generous man..."

"A generous man," the children respond.

"will prosper..."

"will prosper..."

Looks pretty much the same, doesn't it? Not much has changed in two thousand years. But is this the way Jesus would teach? What would it look like if Jesus did teach this way? Let's switch the scene again, this time to Jesus with his disciples at the Last Supper.

Jesus knew that the Father had put all things under his power and that he had come from God and was returning to God; so he got up from the meal, turned to his disciples and said, "Repeat after me: You must serve one another, for it is right and good."

The disciples responded in unison, "You must serve one another, for it is right and good."

"Again," Jesus said.

"You must serve one another, for it is right and good."

"Again."

The real story is recorded in John 13:1-17. But this facetious version of the passage illustrates the way Jesus' teaching methods differed so radically from other rabbis—and from many of us today. Rather than

"One thing that strikes me is how often we've talked about surprise in the context of what Jesus did when he was teaching people. Surprise is a hard thing to pull off and do well. But that was his technique, in a way—to catch people off guard, to get them kind of unsettled so much that it caused them to continue to pursue whatever they were unsettled about."

—Rick Lawrence

telling the disciples they needed to serve one another, he immersed them in an experience of service—one that would make a lasting impact and would not be easily forgotten.

In their book *Why Nobody Learns Much of Anything at Church: And How to Fix It,* Thom and Joani Schultz spotlight this difference about Jesus when they write:

Jesus immersed people in experiences of all kinds—healing some, feeding others, and casting out demons in still others. He manipulated the weather to teach his disciples a lesson (Matthew 8:23-27).

He loved to teach with the interesting materials around him. He didn't use fill-in-the-blank worksheets. He used dirt, water, wine, clothing, trees, grains of wheat, sheep, goats, boats, nets, fish, little children, and a Roman coin—the paraphernalia of his day.

And Jesus knew people learned by doing. To teach his disciples a lesson on servanthood, he dropped to his knees and began washing their feet. He could have preached an eloquent sermon on servanthood. But he knew the power of experience. He knew his men would best understand if they *experienced* this lesson.[12]

Real understanding comes from experience, not from rote memorization. This does not mean that Scripture memorization is bad. However, to be effective it must include an experience that promotes understanding, application, and lifelong recall of the principle being stated. Because Jesus knew this, his teaching often deviated from the rabbinical norm. And maybe ours should too.

Rabbis...*almost never associated with prostitutes, tax collectors, women, or children.*
Jesus...*often did all of these things.*

As we've already pointed out, the Pharisees of Jesus' day were extraordinarily concerned about remaining "clean" in the eyes of the law, which meant obeying the law in every detail. Remaining "clean" was so important, that the Pharisees even had debates over things like whether it was lawful to eat an egg laid on the Sabbath.[13]

You can imagine, then, how repulsed a Pharisee might be at the thought of hanging out with "sinners" and tax collectors (who were considered traitors to Israel)—handling the same dishes, drinking from the same jar, sitting at the same table. All of these things would most likely be well beyond what any self-respecting rabbi could tolerate.

And then there was the problem of sick people. Remember the parable of the Good Samaritan? The priest and the Levite avoided touching the injured man because doing so might make them unclean. In the Jewish culture of Jesus' day, many would probably consider their actions to be the right thing to do.

But not Jesus. He not only touched the sick (and healed them), he openly enjoyed the company of "sinners." He talked with them, ate with them, celebrated with them. In short, he loved them.

"The intriguing thing to me about this is discovering the cost that Jesus was willing to pay to teach the way he did."

—Rick Lawrence

The other rabbis of Jesus' day didn't appreciate his unorthodox approach to teaching. In Matthew 11:19, Jesus challenges their opinions by saying, "The Son of Man came eating and drinking, and they say, 'Here is a glutton and a drunkard, a friend of tax collectors and "sinners." ' But wisdom is proved right by her actions."

Just as Jesus reached out to the outcasts of his day, so should the church today. In his book, *On Being a Christian,* Hans Küng writes:

[The church must constantly be] aware that its faith is weak, its knowledge dim, its profession of faith halting, that there is not a single sin or failing of which it has not in one way or another been guilty. And though it is true that the church must always dissociate itself from sin, it can never have any excuse for keeping any sinners at a distance. If the Church self-righteously remains aloof from failures, irreligious and immoral people, it cannot enter justified into God's kingdom. But if it is constantly aware of its guilt and sin, it can live in the joyous assurance of forgiveness. The promise has been given to it that anyone who humbles himself will be exalted.[14]

One pastor I know tells a story about a man in a small town who committed a sin, and the whole community found out about it. As a result, the man was excommunicated from his church.

The man complained to God, "Lord, they won't let me in because I'm a sinner."

The Lord responded, "What are you complaining about? They won't let me in either."

As a teacher, Jesus never rejected students who had bad reputations or had committed sinful acts in the past. And although this choice invited criticism from other teachers, Jesus did it anyway—for the sake of those he was trying to reach.

That should be our motivation too. As teachers who are striving to be like Jesus, maybe it's time we ask ourselves, "When was the last time we were accused of being friends with 'sinners'?"

Rabbis...*never chose their own disciples. Rather, students chose which rabbi they wanted to study under.*

Jesus...*selected his own disciples.*

For students in Jesus' day, choosing a rabbi to follow was rather like choosing a college (or a major) in today's world. Students back then would listen to the teachings of several rabbis, then decide which teacher they most wanted to emulate, and, if they were "accepted," become his student.

It works that way in today's colleges, too. Students review what several different schools (or majors) have to offer, then choose one that most interests them. Every now and then, however, that system is reversed. If a university finds an exceptionally gifted student (either academically or athletically), the school may actively pursue that person, offering lots of perks to get them to come, such as free tuition, free housing, or even a small stipend.

That example may help us understand how unusual Jesus' approach to choosing his disciples really was. Now, we know that none of the disciples possessed obvious qualities that would compel a rabbi to chase them down. But Jesus called each of them as though they were each exceptional and special. By calling them out and choosing them individually, Jesus extended to them great honor. It's as if he were saying, "I see something special in you. You may look like an ordinary person, but you have extraordinary potential. I want you to join me."

In fact, Jesus said something like this to his disciples in the last days of his life. His words are recorded in John 15:16: "You did not choose me, but I chose you and appointed you to go and bear fruit—fruit that will last. Then the Father will give you whatever you ask in my name."

As Christians, we, too, are "chosen" by Jesus and can experience the same deep affirmation of our own value that the original disciples experienced in Christ. In 2 Thessalonians 2:13-14, Paul writes:

"But we ought always to thank God for you, brothers loved by the Lord, because from the beginning God chose you to be saved through the sanctifying work of the Spirit and through belief in the truth. He called you to this through our gospel, that you might share in the glory of our Lord Jesus Christ."

As a teacher, Jesus actively pursued and chose some of those who sat under his teaching. That might have interesting implications for the way we teach today. For example, instead of setting up a class and waiting to see who shows up, maybe our roles as teachers should include actively pursuing people to join our class—to help them feel valued and loved as individuals.

Rabbis...*required their disciples to serve them in various ways, including clearing a path for them in a crowd or helping them put on their sandals.*[15]
Jesus...*called his disciples "friends" and served them instead of letting them serve him (John 13:1-17; 15:14).*

Popular Bible teacher Charles Swindoll has noted that in all of the Gospels, there is only one time Jesus describes his "inner man" in his own words. The two words he chooses, says Swindoll, are not "phenomenal and great," "wise and powerful," or "holy and eternal." The two words are "gentle" and "humble."

"Come to me, all you who are weary and burdened, and I will give you rest. Take my yoke upon you and learn from me, for I am gentle and humble in heart, and you will find rest for your souls" (Matthew 11:28-29).

Swindoll adds that those are "servant" words.[16] But they're also "teacher" words. Did you catch what he says just before he uses those words? "Take my yoke upon you and *learn* from me" (author emphasis). For Jesus, having the attitude of a servant was at the heart of what it meant to be a teacher. That was probably why he didn't allow his disciples to fawn all over him the way the disciples of other rabbis did. That kind of superior attitude didn't fit who he was.

And as Christian teachers, it shouldn't fit who we are either. Paul sums up how Christ's example applies to us when he writes:

"Your attitude should be the same as that of Christ Jesus: Who, being in very nature God, did not consider equality with God something to be grasped, but made himself nothing, taking the very nature of a servant" (Philippians 2:5-7a).

An attitude of pure, undiluted servanthood formed the bedrock of Christ's heart as a teacher. That same attitude should shape our teaching as well.

Rabbis...allowed their disciples to become rabbis themselves, once their training was complete.

Jesus...taught his disciples that he was the only true Teacher, so they should never call themselves "rabbi" (Matthew 23:8).

Jesus makes this shocking statement in Matthew 23:8, where he states: "But you are not to be called 'Rabbi,' for you have only one Master and you are all brothers."

A statement like this must have floored the disciples! In today's terms, it would be like a university professor standing before his class of college seniors and declaring, "Sorry, but I'm never going to let you graduate from this class. I've decided it's best for me to remain your teacher for the rest of your lives. I will be your teacher, and you will all be classmates to one another until you die."

Talk about an academic nightmare! But that's not far off the mark of what Jesus did with his disciples. The accepted educational course for new rabbis was to sit under the instruction of a respected rabbi, then eventually be accepted as a rabbi yourself. Jesus outright rejected this educational structure and instructed his disciples never to rely on their own wisdom or the titles given by men, but rather to always look to him as the one true Teacher of us all.

In the same way, we should never make the mistake of believing that we can accomplish anything as teachers outside of the wisdom and guidance of God's Spirit. He is the true Teacher—we are not. Apart from his guidance and power working through us, our teaching is useless (John 15:5).

A Few Similarities

Despite all the ways Jesus' teaching style differed from his rabbinical counterparts, there were also several ways Jesus embraced the rabbinical style of teaching. For example:

- Jesus chose to lead a small group of disciples, just as the rabbis did (Matthew 4:18-22; John 1:35-51).
- Jesus frequently quoted the Old Testament to support his teaching, as did the rabbis (Mark 7:6-7; 12:10-11, 28-33).
- Jesus sometimes taught in synagogues, just like the rabbis (Matthew 9:35; 13:54; Luke 4:15; 6:6).
- Jesus often taught in parables, which was common among rabbis (Matthew 13:24-43; Luke 14:16-24).
- Jesus used aphorisms (quick, easy-to-remember statements that point out a truth or principle), as did the rabbis (Matthew 10:39; 12:37).
- Jesus entered into debates over religious matters, as did the rabbis (Matthew 12:1-8; 19:3-9).

Some might say that Jesus did these rabbi-like things because of the culture he lived in. For this reason, they say, we shouldn't assume that Jesus would use these same practices or methods if he were teaching on earth today—in our culture. But we've already clearly seen that Jesus had no trouble breaking cultural norms to make his teaching more effective. So it's probably more likely that Jesus followed these particular rabbinical teaching practices because they worked—and for no other reason.

Jesus was the greatest teacher who ever lived. Even though he broke from the norm for rabbis in so many ways, the real impact of his teaching wasn't based on his unconventional methods—rather, it was the *message* Christ brought that shook the world.

Though many of Jesus' contemporaries didn't approve of what he taught, they could not deny the impact his message had on people. In fact, the teachings Jesus gave held such potent truth that they couldn't be refuted by the rest of the teaching community. The only way the teachers of the law could stop Jesus' teaching was by killing him. And so they did.

During his last days on earth, Jesus made a startling statement to his disciples—a simple, powerful truth that continues to apply to us today.

"Remember the words I spoke to you: 'No servant is greater than his master.' If they persecuted me, they will persecute you also. If they obeyed my teaching, they will obey yours also" (John 15:20).

That statement provides the ultimate "litmus test" for our authenticity as teachers of the good news of Jesus Christ. The Rabbi Jesus Christ taught his disciples in ways that surprised and even shocked the leaders of his day. He sifted through the respected educational philosophies and methods of the rabbis, rejected some, added others, and turned many of them upside down. He didn't do this to make people angry (even though that did happen). He did things differently because, as a teacher, he knew what would *work*. And he was absolutely committed to teaching in a way that made a permanent impact. You might even say his life depended on it.

As a result, he started a revolution. And his students went on to change the world.

"In this time period in history involving these few people, and without the media and technology or anything we have today, it is just so miraculous! Only God could do this—I mean, it's so miraculous that we are sitting in this room today because of what happened two thousand years ago."

—Joani Schultz

In later chapters, we'll more closely examine each of the teaching methods we've highlighted in this chapter and discover how we can effectively translate each one into our own teaching today. But before we do that, there are just a few more questions we must answer:

• What was Christ's goal as a teacher?

• How can we translate that goal into our teaching today?

In the next chapter, we'll discover the answer to these questions and more.

[1] New Bible Dictionary, Second Edition (Downers Grove, IL: InterVarsity Press, 1982), 1006.

[2] Roy B. Zuck, *Teaching as Jesus Taught* (Grand Rapids, MI: Baker Books, 1995), 35.

[3] New Bible Dictionary, Second Edition, 1006.

[4] New International Dictionary of New Testament Theology quoted in *Teaching as Jesus Taught,* 27.

[5] New Bible Dictionary, Second Edition, 1006.

[6] Zuck, *Teaching as Jesus Taught,* 24. The only other title for Jesus that occurred more frequently than teacher was "Son of Man," which Jesus used in reference to himself.

[7] Ibid., 24.

[8] John P. Kealy, *Jesus, the Teacher* (Denville, NJ: Dimension, 1978), 11. Quoted in *Teaching as Jesus Taught.*

[9] New Bible Dictionary, Second Edition, 924-925.

[10] Ralph Gower, *The New Manners and Customs of Bible Times* (Chicago, IL: Moody Press, 1987), 257.

[11] Ibid., 258.

[12] Thom and Joani Schultz, *Why Nobody Learns Much of Anything at Church: And How to Fix It* (Loveland, CO: Group Publishing, 1993), 118.

[13] Gower, *The New Manners and Customs of Bible Times,* 257.

[14] Hans Küng, *On Being a Christian,* (Garden City, NY: Doubleday & Co., 1976), 507-508.

[15] Zuck, *Teaching as Jesus Taught,* 41.

[16] Charles R. Swindoll, *Improving Your Serve,* (Waco, TX: Word, Inc., 1981), 162.

Chapter 3
Why Jesus Taught

"Now this is eternal life: that they may know you,
the only true God, and Jesus Christ, whom you have sent.
I have brought you glory on earth
by completing the work you gave me to do...
I have revealed you to those whom you gave me out of the world.
They were yours; you gave them to me
and they have obeyed your word...
For I gave them the words you gave me
and they accepted them. They knew with certainty
that I came from you, and they believed
that you sent me."
—John 17:3-4,6,8

Let's say you gathered all the Christians from all the denominations, all the "nondenominations," all the movements, and all the parachurch organizations, and you put them all together in a great hall, and you asked each of them, one by one, point blank: What's the most important thing in the Christian life?

What do you think they would say?

What would you say?

In his book *The Secret to the Christian Life,* Gene Edwards asks a similar question:

What have you been told is the secret to the Christian life? I have asked that question of thousands of Christians all across the English-speaking world, in traditional churches, in home churches, and in conferences: "What were you told you were supposed to do to be a good Christian?"...Do you recognize the answers I received back?...I present them here more or less in descending order:

Pray and read your Bible

Go to church

Witness...

Tithe

Do these sound familiar? They are the most frequently heard. But here are more!

Serve the Lord

Go to Sunday school

Learn positional truth

Learn the exchanged life

Go to a Christian college

Go to a Bible school

Go to the seminary

Learn the faith-walk life

Learn the faith-rest life

There are yet more: spiritual warfare, submission and authority, miracles, powers, obeying prophecy, reclaiming the gifts, head covering, peculiar dress, strict morals, (even) vegetarianism, becoming a covenant people, and the ever familiar "join our group because we are *it*."[1]

It's modern day mayhem. As teachers and leaders in the church, we very often present such a cacophony of opinions and conflicting priorities that all the world can usually hear is the static of our dissonant voices scraping together.

And it's no better within the church walls. If what churchgoers (that is, our *students)* are saying is any indication, it seems we may not really know *what* exactly we should be teaching or *how* we should teach it or really even *why* we're teaching in the first place.

One pastor I know recently related a story about a young girl who had made the decision to become a Christian. But because she had not been raised in any church, she was unsure about the Bible's instructions concerning baptism. On the advice of a friend, she called the pastor and asked him to meet with her and explain the church's beliefs.

The pastor agreed and brought with him a booklet on baptism that his church had prepared for just such occasions. When they met, the pastor guided the young lady through the booklet, explaining the points as he went. When he finished, he asked, "Do you have any questions?"

"Well, yeah," the girl said. She then pulled out a whole stack of similar booklets put together by other churches in the area. "What you're saying sounds good," she continued, "but what each of these other churches says sounds good, too. Which one am I supposed to believe?"

In the end, the girl was more confused than ever. Now I'm not saying the church shouldn't hold to any beliefs concerning baptism—of course we should. But when this girl was finished trying to discover what it means to obey Jesus, do you think she was any closer to understanding than when she started? Probably not. After all, if we as teachers don't agree about what's really important in the Christian faith, how can we expect our students to learn anything? As Thom and Joani Schultz have written, "Without a clearly defined goal we'll waffle and never 'win the prize.' But if our educational goal is a good one that's apparent to everyone, we'll change lives with the power of the Lord."[2]

"One Lord, One Faith...": A Unified Goal

Astronaut Michael Collins, who orbited the moon while Neil Armstrong took those historic steps on its surface, has written an account of what it was like to see the earth from space for the first time.

> I think the view from 100,000 miles could be invaluable in getting people together to work out joint solutions, by causing them to realize that the planet we share unites us in a way far more basic and far more important than differences in skin color or religion or economic system. That all-important border would be invisible, that noisy argument suddenly silenced. The tiny globe would continue to turn, serenely ignoring its subdivisions, presenting a unified facade that would cry out for unified understanding, for homogeneous treatment. The earth *must* become as it appears: blue and white, not capitalist or Communist; blue and white, not rich or poor; blue and white, not envious or envied...There is but one earth, tiny and fragile, and one must get 100,000 miles away from it to appreciate fully one's good fortune in living on it.[3]

In a way, Michael Collins and Jesus Christ have something in common. When Michael returned to earth, he brought with him a fresh, powerful perspective on the fundamental unity we all share as human beings. We are all made by the same Creator, and we all share the same space, with resources that God has provided to help us live together peacefully. Underneath our bank accounts or the color of our skin, we are all made of the same stuff, and the lines we draw between us seem to lose all meaning when we take a step back and look at the world from this astronaut's perspective.

When Jesus came to earth, he came from a perspective that's much higher and far more complete than even Michael Collins (or any of us) can possibly imagine. Because of his immutable understanding of everything that is, Jesus *knows* the goal of life. He came to teach us about true life—really, to teach us that he *is* true life—and when he taught, his teaching was never cluttered with contradictory objectives or conflicting opinions. He didn't allow himself to get caught up in debates that ultimately didn't matter.

Rick Yount put it this way. "Jesus majored on truth, the Pharisees on trivia. Jesus majored on love, the Pharisees on legalism. Jesus majored on justice, the Pharisees on judgment."[4] Jesus cut through the fringe issues and focused on the real goal—and his teaching changed the world.

The task of teaching people about Jesus has now fallen into our hands. Jesus never wanted the confusion we see in the ranks of Christian teachers today. He wants our teaching to be unified, simple, and focused on the goal—just like his. In his final prayer to the Father before his death, he made his heart's desire perfectly clear.

"My prayer is not for them alone. I pray also for those who will believe in me through their message, that all of them may be one, Father, just as you are in me and I am in you. May they also be in us so that the world may believe that you have sent me. I have given them the glory that you gave me, that they may be one as we are one: I in them and you in me. May they be brought to complete unity to let the world know that you sent me and have loved them even as you have loved me" (John 17:20-23).

The Apostle Paul echoed Christ's desire when he wrote:

"If you have any encouragement from being united with Christ, if any comfort from his love, if any fellowship with the Spirit, if any tenderness and compassion, then make my joy complete by being like-minded, having the same love, being one in spirit and purpose" (Philippians 2:1-2).

If we are to be teachers who follow in Jesus' steps, then we must align ourselves with Jesus the same way he was aligned with the Father. We must understand and commit ourselves to the same goal Jesus had as a teacher. We must know the overriding "point" of his teaching ministry on earth.

The Main Thing

As I mentioned in the introduction, many of the insights contained in this book were gleaned from weeks of discussion and intensive study by a team of educators and leaders that I had the privilege of working with for many years. As we embarked together to uncover the goal of Christ's teaching, we quickly discovered that Jesus' goal was not as clear cut as it might first appear. Jesus encountered a wide variety of people, each with unique needs and unique potential. He responded in a personal way to each person he encountered. He challenged some and rebuked others. He offered calm forgiveness to the woman at the well and violently overturned the tables of the money-changers at the temple. He often harshly rebuked the Pharisees, but was typically gentle when teaching more ordinary folks like Mary and Martha.

After several weeks of investigation, our study group finally had to ask: Since Jesus employed such a variety of techniques and objectives in his teaching, is it possible to find one place in Scripture where we can clearly see the overriding goal of all that Jesus taught?

The answer we discovered? Absolutely, yes! Christine Yount, editor of Children's Ministry Magazine, brought that goal into focus one day when she said, "There's this huge goal that spans the ages, and if you want to boil it down to 'When Jesus taught, what was his goal?', I think that's possible. And I keep coming back to John 17."

Let's take a closer look at this key passage to see if we can uncover the "one goal" that guided everything Jesus did as a teacher.

To begin, let's set the scene. It was just hours before Jesus' arrest—probably the most emotionally intense time of his life on earth. Jesus' personal anguish over what he was about to face was so profound that the Bible says, "His sweat was like drops of blood falling to the ground" (Luke 22:44b). His concern wasn't only for his own life—the pain of his coming crucifixion and the far greater agony of taking the world's sin onto himself. It was also for his followers, who were soon to be like "scattered sheep" with no shepherd (Matthew 26:31).[5]

In these final hours, Jesus lays out his heart before the Father. He reveals his pain, reaffirms his faith, and sums up the purpose of all that he has said or done during his time on earth. Let's take a look inside the heart of our Savior...

"Father, the time has come. Glorify your Son, that your Son may glorify you. For you granted him authority over all people that he might give eternal life to all those you have given him. Now this is eternal life: that they may know you, the only true God, and Jesus Christ, whom you have sent. I have brought you glory on earth by completing the work you gave me to do. And now, Father, glorify me in your presence with the glory I had with you before the world began. I have revealed you to those whom you gave me out of the world. They were yours; you gave them to me and they have obeyed your word. Now they know that everything you have given me comes from you. For I gave them the words you gave me and they accepted them. They knew with certainty that I came from you, and they believed that you sent me" (John 17:1b-8).

Twice in this prayer, Jesus states the "ultimate" goal that guided his teaching (and everything else he did, for that matter). Can you find the statements? Here they are:

- "For you granted him authority over all people that he might give eternal life to all those you have given him. Now this is eternal life: that they may know you, the only true God, and Jesus Christ, whom you have sent" (John 17:2-3).
- "I have revealed you to those whom you gave me out of the world" (John 17:6a).

Since Jesus states his goal slightly different each time, let's take a look at each of these statements separately, then pull them together to come up with one overall teaching goal for Christ's ministry.

In the opening sentence of these verses, Jesus states that his purpose was to "give eternal life" to all those God had given him. But what is eternal life? And what does Jesus mean by saying that he gives eternal life to those God *has given him?*

Jesus answers the first question himself in the very next statement. He says, "Now this is eternal life: that they may know you, the only true God, and Jesus Christ, whom you have sent." The word translated "know" is the Greek word *ginōskō*. The word means "to understand completely" and conveys the picture of an intimate union, as between man and woman.[6] So then, Jesus came to give people a way to know God (and himself) intimately.

But what about the second question? The answer lies in Principle 1. You remember Principle 1, don't you?

Principle 1
Realize that people cannot understand truth unless God enables them.

People cannot understand God's truth unless God gives them the ability. And God won't give them the ability to understand unless their hearts are humble and open (see Proverbs 3:34). So Jesus is saying in essence that his goal was targeted specifically at those whose hearts were already open to God.

Let's see if the second statement Christ makes sheds any additional light on his goal: "I have revealed you to those whom you gave me out of the world" (John 17:6a). Once again, Jesus clarifies that his goal is to "reveal" God to those whom God has called. The word "reveal" here signifies to "uncover" or "unveil"[7] and is the same word Jesus used when he praised Peter for recognizing that he was the Christ (see Matthew 16:17). The context suggests that Jesus is speaking of a personal revelation, reinforcing the notion that eternal life means "knowing" God in a personal way.

Based on these two statements, we can now effectively sum up Jesus' goal as a teacher. We'll list it here as the primary principle for teaching the way Jesus taught.

Principle 2
The ultimate goal of Christian teaching is to draw people into a genuine, personal relationship with God.

That's quite a simple, yet powerful goal, isn't it? But it raises a few questions, such as "How do we accomplish this goal?" and "How can we tell whether we're achieving this goal?"

The rest of this book is dedicated to answering the question of how we can carry out Jesus' goal effectively and practically in modern times, but let me just highlight one other statement Jesus makes in this passage that hits on that particular issue. The passage says, "For I gave them the words you gave me and they accepted them" (John 17:8a). This statement provides us with a simple (but not necessarily easy) plumb line for determining whether or not we're going about the "how" of teaching as Jesus taught in the right way. Jesus' statement describes a simple transaction between God, himself, and the disciples. Taken in context, this transaction is based on a strong intimacy between the Father and Jesus, and it focuses the teaching on the *Father's* words—not Christ's words. In an earlier passage in John, Jesus says, "For I did not speak of my own accord, but the Father who sent me commanded me what to say and how to say it" (John 12:49). In the same way, our teaching must be founded on a strong personal intimacy with God through the Spirit and focused on God's Word instead of our own. The goal is to teach *God's* Word. Unless we understand and consistently apply this truth in following Christ's goal as a teacher, all of our own teaching efforts will be pointless.

Teacher's Corner: Promoting Your Goal

Once you know the goal of your teaching, how can you promote it among all the people in your church? Thom and Joani Schultz make these suggestions:

- Print it in the church bulletin, preceding each week's calendar of educational offerings.
- Decorate colorful bulletin boards that splash your goal on the walls of your church.
- Display it at the top of each committee's agenda for each meeting.
- Paste stickers with your goal on each teachers manual.
- Create fun buttons that broadcast your goal for leadership, teachers, and parents to wear.
- Incorporate your goal into your church's annual report to remind members of your direction.
- Create long computer-printed banners of your goal to hang in every classroom.

- Place it on a schedule board that lists the church's educational options.
- Put it in your church brochure (if you have one) to let new members learn about your goal.[8]

Measuring Our Success

Here's the second question Christ's goal raises for us: "How can we tell when we've succeeded at the goal? In this same passage, Jesus also reveals four evidences (or outcomes) that can serve to tell us whether we're on the right track when it comes to achieving our ultimate goal as teachers. Consider these:

- **Your students will trust in Jesus (John 17:8).** Jesus is the rock of our salvation and the only way to true relationship with the Father. If our teaching conveys this truth so that our students put their trust in Jesus, we will know we have been successful as teachers.

- **Your students will obey God's Word (John 17:6).** One of the easiest ways to tell that our teaching is effective is when it bears fruit in our students' lives. When people obey God's Word as a result of our teaching, we will know we have been successful.

- **Your students will recognize that everything you have comes from God (John 17:7).** This may seem like an odd "outcome" at first, but it's actually a strong indicator of our genuineness as teachers. We've all listened to teachers and speakers who may have had great things to say, but who were ultimately interested in glorifying themselves rather than God. Jesus made it clear that he did not seek glory for himself (John 8:50), but all of his words and actions sought to bring glory to the Father (John 7:18). In the same way, when our teaching points people to God as the source of our life and instruction, we will know we have been successful.

- **Your teaching will bring glory to God (John 17:4).** Jesus brought glory to God by completing the work God had sent him to do. So we, too, will be successful teachers as we practice total obedience to God's commands and remain true to God's Word in all that we teach and do. In doing this, we will know we are successful.

Did Jesus achieve all of these outcomes with everyone he taught? No, of course not—and neither will we. But when we examine the overall impact of our efforts as Christian teachers, these fruits should be evident in those whose hearts are humble and receptive—just as they were evident in Christ's disciples.

Sometimes seeing real evidence of successful teaching takes time—even a long time. Dick Gruber, a children's pastor in Minnesota, tells a story about the "evidence" he witnessed in one young boy named Lance.

Two and a half years ago when I met Lance, he was the ringleader in a plot to ruin the children's church. He was bored, restless, and very creative. It was obvious to me from the beginning that this boy was a child of higher intelligence and a leader of others. So I began to pay attention to him *before* he caused big problems.

For two years, I kept reminding Lance of who he was. I referred to him at every opportunity as "Lance, leader of men."

Last summer God got a hold of Lance. He's now a sixth grader. Lance, leader of men, is one of the most positive guys you'll ever pray to have in your children's church.[9]

Some of Jesus' disciples took even longer to come around. We're all familiar with the story of Thomas, who would not believe in Jesus' resurrection until he saw the evidence for himself. And we know about Peter, who actually denied that he even knew Jesus, much less that he was a follower. From Peter's writings and other historical records, we know that both of these men went on to do great things for God.[10]

The Apostle Paul was also pretty slow to come around. Although there is no clear evidence that Paul was acquainted with Jesus during his earthly ministry, some scholars believe Paul actually grew up in Jerusalem (see Acts 22:3), and was most likely, therefore, personally exposed to much of Jesus' teaching. If that's true, then Paul's conversion to Christianity occurred

> *"Jesus wasn't here just to heal the blind man or to raise Lazarus from the dead or even to teach five thousand people about how to live better lives. He was here to establish a beginning for something that would be further built on, into what—to some degree at least—Christianity is today. To try to pin down Jesus' teaching in terms of the effect that it had on the people of his day isn't enough. I really think we need to look at it in terms of what his intent was while he was there; the effect that it would have on people as it was processed through that generation and the next."*
> —Paul Woods

only after being exposed to Christ's teaching for over six years.[11]

So don't lose heart if you don't see immediate results in your efforts to teach as Jesus taught. It took time for Jesus to train his disciples in God's ways. It will take time for us to do it, too. But eventually, if we remain faithful, we will see good fruit come from our teaching.

Goals Within the Goal

Everything Jesus did or said can be traced to his overriding goal. But other goals can be seen as well. In her book *How Jesus Taught,* Regina M. Alfonso describes how Jesus' techniques and goals as a teacher shifted according to the type of "student" he dealt with. In fact, Alfonso cites at least eleven different student types that Jesus taught. These include:

- the insecure student (John 5:1-18),
- the experimenter (Matthew 14:28-33),
- the eager student (Mark 10:17-21),
- the discouraged student (Luke 24:13-35),
- the humiliated student (John 8:1-11),
- the masked student (John 4:1-30),
- the persevering searcher (Mark 17:40-41,47),
- the unpopular, unaccepted student (Matthew 8:1-4),
- the gifted student (John 3:1-12),
- the crafty student (Luke 19:1-9), and
- the shy student (Mark 5:25-34).[12]

With each of these types of students, Jesus' objective and technique altered to fit the need of the moment. In our classrooms today, we need to know our students and adapt our teaching methods according to the type of learner we are dealing with. Our quest as Christian teachers is to learn not only how and why Jesus chose his objectives, but also how we can translate them into our own teaching—while remaining true to the main goal of leading people into genuine, personal relationships with God.

For the purposes of our investigation, we'll reduce Alfonso's list into two primary categories of learners: Disciples and Seekers. Disciples refer to those who have already made a life-commitment to love, follow, and obey Jesus, while Seekers refer to those whose hearts are open and curious, but are as yet unconvinced to follow Christ.

In addition, we'll also consider a third group that Jesus dealt with.

We might call this "the unteachable student." But we'll adopt the title used by the Apostle Luke in Luke 13:17, where he calls them simply "opponents." They were people who resisted Jesus' teaching, either through active aggression against Christ or passive rejection of his teaching.

Objectives for Disciples

When Jesus cursed the fig tree in front of his disciples, what was his objective as a teacher? When Jesus invited Peter to walk on the water, what lesson was he trying to convey? When Jesus didn't respond to Mary and Martha's request until after Lazarus was dead, what was his point?

Pinpointing Jesus' specific objectives with each of his disciples can seem daunting at first. In fact, it can be like trying to identify all the goals a parent might pursue during the early years of a child's life—weaning, potty training, walking, eating with a spoon, mastering language, playing fair...the list goes on. But as with parenting, when we look at the "big picture" of Jesus' teaching objectives for his disciples, four major themes begin to emerge. We'll consider each in more or less the order of its apparent importance in Jesus' ministry:

• **Objective 1: To build relationships.**

Since Jesus' ultimate goal was to draw people into relationships with the Father, it only makes sense that he would focus much of his teaching on helping his disciples build relationships with himself—and with each other.

His teaching often focused on powerful relational qualities, such as forgiveness (Luke 15:11-32) and mercy (Matthew 18:23-34). And his lifestyle demonstrated acceptance (John 8:1-11), friendship (John 11:17-44), and love (John 19:28-30). Jesus was a relational Savior—the Son of a relational God.

Two scenes in particular that reveal Jesus' passion for relationships are found in John 13:33-35 and John 17: 9-11. The first records some of Jesus' final words to his disciples. The second records some of his last words to the Father.

Let's take a look at both of these passages in turn. As you read them, think about what sort of passion in Christ's heart would spur him to say these things.

"My children, I will be with you only a little longer. You will look for me, and just as I told the Jews, so I tell you now: Where I am going, you cannot come. A new command I give you: Love one another. As I have loved you, so you must love one another. By this all men will know that you are my disciples, if you love one another" (John 13:33-35).

"I pray for them. I am not praying for the world, but for those you have given me, for they are yours. All I have is yours, and all you have is mine. And glory has come to me through them. I will remain in the world no longer, but they are still in the world, and I am coming to you. Holy Father, protect them by the power of your name—the name you gave me—so that they may be one as we are one" (John 17:9-11).

Jesus' passion was for us to be one in unity as his followers. Even today, he still longs for his disciples to love one another, just as he has loved us. In fact, teaching people to love each other was so important in Jesus' teaching that one time he even included it as a part of the main goal. Listen to how he responded to the Pharisee who asked, "What is the greatest commandment?"

"Jesus replied, 'Love the Lord your God with all your heart and with all your soul and with all your mind.' This is the first and greatest commandment. And the second is like it: 'Love your neighbor as yourself' " (Matthew 22:37-39).

When it comes to disciples, the first objective of all teaching is to build genuine relationships in the bond of authentic love.

• **Objective 2: To train in love.**

Closely related to the first objective is this second "subgoal" of Jesus' teaching: to teach people how to love. To teach this objective, Jesus did not stand at the front of the class, draw charts and diagrams, and expound on the principles upon which love is built. Instead, he "lived love"—right in front of his disciples...or, more accurately, right *toward* them. He demonstrated what it means to love, what it costs to love, and what is gained from love. In this way, his objective was not only to help his disciples build relationships, but also to learn how to love each other well in the midst of those relationships.

It is only because of Christ's example that C. S. Lewis had the insight to write the following:

Love anything and your heart will be wrung and possibly broken. If you want to make sure of keeping it intact you must give it to no one, not even an animal. Wrap it carefully round with hobbies and little luxuries; avoid all entanglements. Lock it up safe in the casket or coffin of your selfishness. But in that casket—safe, dark, motionless, airless—it will change. It will not be broken; it will become unbreakable, impenetrable, irredeemable.[13]

As Christian educators, we are not called to "avoid all entanglements." In fact, quite the opposite is true. Adopting Jesus' objectives in the way we teach his followers will require us to let go of our "separateness" and love them boldly.

Teaching others to love in this way won't be easy. And it will cost us. Dr. Dan B. Allender defines this kind of bold love as *"a sacrifice for the undeserving that opens the door to restoration of relationship with the Father, with others, and with ourselves."*

But, Allender goes on to say, "It is in the light of Christ's sacrificial, intentional, and transforming love that we are to define love. It is equally on this basis that we will be evaluated and, one day, judged."[14]

● **Objective 3: To train in faith and obedience.**

One cynic has defined faith as "belief without evidence in what is told by one who speaks without knowledge of things without parallel."[15]

Quite to the contrary of this cynic's opinion, Jesus' disciples grew in faith because of the evidence they did see (not lack of it). They grew in their belief in Christ because Jesus' words came with authority (not "without knowledge"). And although Jesus did teach his disciples many amazing things, he almost always did it by drawing parallels to simple, understandable real-life situations.

Helping students grow in faith toward God is another of Christ's objectives that we must embrace as teachers who follow in his steps. At first glance, it may seem like an impossible goal to measure. After all, how can we tell whether a student is growing in faith?

The answer is more simple than you might think. The truth is that we can tell whether a person is living by faith simply by watching the way he or she lives. As James puts it:

"What good is it, my brothers, if a man claims to have faith but has no deeds? Can such faith save him? Suppose a brother or sister is without clothes and daily food. If one of you says to him, 'Go, I wish you well; keep warm and well fed,' but does nothing about his physical needs, what good is it? In the same way, faith by itself, if it is not accompanied by action, is dead" (James 2:14-17).

Jesus said, "If you love me, you will obey what I command" (John 14:15). As our students grow in their love for God and learn to trust him more, the result will be a consistent obedience to God's Word.

In Luke 12:42-48, Jesus relates a parable about the importance of faithful obedience in a disciple's life. As you read it, think about how this parable reveals Jesus' interest in teaching his disciples about faith and obedience to God. Then read it again, this time thinking about how this story might apply to you as a teacher today.

"Who then is the faithful and wise manager, whom the master puts in charge of his servants to give them their food allowance at the proper time? It will be good for that servant whom the master finds doing so when he returns. I tell you the truth, he will put him in charge of all his possessions. But suppose the servant says to himself, 'My master is taking a long time in coming,' and he then begins to beat the menservants and maidservants and to eat and drink and get drunk. The master of that servant will come on a day when he does not expect him and at an hour he is not aware of. He will cut him to pieces and assign him a place with the unbelievers.

"That servant who knows his master's will and does not get ready or does not do what his master wants will be beaten with many blows. But the one who does not know and does things deserving punishment will be beaten with few blows. From everyone who has been given much, much will be demanded; and from the one who has been entrusted with much, much more will be asked" (Luke 12:42-48).

In a later passage, James issues this warning: "Not many of you should presume to be teachers, my brothers, because you know that we who teach will be judged more strictly" (James 3:1). I don't know if James was thinking back to this parable as he wrote those words, but I wouldn't be surprised. And it shouldn't surprise us, either, to know that when Jesus returns he will want to know not whether we taught about faith and obedience with our words, but whether we taught it with our lives. Just as he did.

• Objective 4: To send in boldness.

One pastor relates the story of a time he was called to the hospital late at night to visit a sick patient. As he walked down the sterile hallway, a man whom he'd never seen before bounded out of one of the rooms. He ran up to the pastor with joy on his face and said, "She's going to make it. She's better. She is going to make it!" And then he made his way on down the hall. The pastor never saw the man again after that night. He had no idea who "she" was, but could only assume she was someone very dear to him, and that he could not wait to share the good news about her. The man didn't even have to know the person with whom he shared it; it just poured out of him—as good news should.[16]

As a master teacher, Jesus understood that the "good news" he had been teaching was meant to be shared. In fact, if his disciples could not or would not share the message he had taught them, it would have revealed that they really had not learned it in the first place. Good news like that is meant to be shared.

So in Luke 9:1-6, Jesus commissioned his disciples for a short-term mission project. We must remember that these men were still very much in training with Christ and were barely capable of standing on their own without him there. But he sent them out to give them the chance to solidify their learning by putting it into practice in the real world. So the disciples set out, without their teacher, to assess what they had learned.

"When Jesus had called the Twelve together, he gave them power and authority to drive out all demons and to cure diseases, and he sent them out to preach the kingdom of God and to heal the sick. He told them: 'Take nothing for the journey—no staff, no bag, no bread, no money, no extra tunic. Whatever house you enter, stay there until you leave that town. If people do not welcome you, shake the dust off your feet when you leave their town, as a testimony against them.' So they set out and went from village to village, preaching the gospel and healing people everywhere" (Luke 9:1-6).

As teachers, we're often so concerned about helping our students succeed that we're afraid to let them fail. But Jesus did not teach in this way. To test the quality of his own teaching, he sent his disciples out for "lab time" in the real world, *without* him there to watch over them. He wouldn't even allow the disciples to take along any personal "crutches"—no bag, bread, money, or extra clothes. Their success depended wholly on how well they had learned the lessons Jesus taught. For Jesus, it was a risky way of assessing learning. But it was also necessary, because he knew he wouldn't always be there in the flesh to watch over them. And he knew in the future they would face far worse than a few jeering crowds.

This form of assessment is necessary for our teaching, too. There is no crucible for learning that's as effective as real-life experience. And to teach as Jesus taught, we must be willing to place our students "out there" where they can risk genuine failure and experience genuine success. (In Chapter 6, we'll look more closely at how we can effectively use experiences as both a learning tool and an assessment tool in our teaching.)

Teacher's Corner:
The Role of Risk in Assessment With Children

The willingness to allow students to fail in order to assess their learning may sound good when talking about youth or adults. But what about children? Should children be exempt from this sort of "bold" assessment because letting them fail so publicly could damage their self-esteem?

Christine Yount, editor of Group's Children's Ministry Magazine, offers these thoughts:

"The greatest risk in assessment with children is that we might not do it— that we might never know whether this generation of children is 'getting it' for today and for tomorrow.

"The idea that children's fragile self-esteem will be dashed by assessment comes out of the misguided belief that the more we tell children how wonderful they are, the more they'll believe it—even if their performance contradicts the cheerleader's message. 'Yea, you!' we scream from the sidelines of life while kids shake their heads and wonder why we don't see the truth about the times that they give us a mediocre offering of something that they are oh-so-much-more capable of.

"The greatest self-esteem booster is to follow Jesus' example with his disciples. Jesus modeled what he expected of his disciples, and he gave them plenty of time to catch on. Then he sent them out to carry out the same tasks. We, too, can equip children for challenging and meaningful tasks that will enable them to change their world. As we enable them to be successful in the things of God, we build their self-esteem."

Objectives for Seekers

We don't stop being Seekers when we become Disciples. If anything, our seeking only intensifies after coming to Christ. That's because our seeking now has a focus—Jesus—and we go after him with our whole being. Consequently, the goals Jesus had in teaching Seekers also apply to Disciples. But as we'll see in the following examples, Jesus focused on the following objectives more often when he dealt with Seekers than when he was teaching his Disciples. Again, we'll list them roughly in the order of their importance.

• **Objective 1: To encourage in faith.**

Jesus cared about Seekers. Much of his time was spent reaching out to and teaching the crowds that would gather to see him. And very often, Jesus' actions would make quite an impression on people's lives. Take a look at these verses:

"Jesus went throughout Galilee, teaching in their synagogues, preaching the good news of the kingdom, and healing every disease and sickness among the people. News about him spread all over Syria, and people brought to him all who were ill with various diseases, those suffering severe pain, the demon-possessed, those having seizures, and the paralyzed, and he healed them. Large crowds from Galilee, the Decapolis, Jerusalem, Judea and the region across the Jordan followed him" (Matthew 4:23-25).

"Great crowds came to him, bringing the lame, the blind, the crippled, the mute and many others, and laid them at his feet; and he healed them" (Matthew 15:30).

"For he had healed many, so that those with diseases were pushing forward to touch him" (Mark 3:10).

Obviously, healing was an important aspect of Jesus' ministry. But why did Jesus heal? Of course, Scripture makes it clear that one reason Jesus healed was because he was motivated by compassion (Matthew 14:14). But, *as a teacher*, what was Jesus' motive for healing and performing other miracles?

I believe it was to encourage faith (see John 20:30-31). By this I do not mean that Jesus performed miracles only to provoke faith in those who had

"[Jesus'] goal was to bring people into relationship or union with God. That made Jesus controversial then and now because the people of his time were looking for a kind of Messiah to relieve them of the political nasties that were going on there. But it's not really what he was about. Even the physical healings that he did were a means to the ultimate goal of directing people back to a relationship with God."

—Thom Schultz

none (see Matthew 4:1-11). Rather, I mean he also healed the sick to encourage and inspire the faith they already had. Several times in Scripture Jesus said to those he had healed, "Go in peace; your faith has healed you." They experienced God's power because they believed. Consequently, their faith was strengthened even more.

As teachers in our complicated modern world, we may not be called to heal the sick or perform miracles in the way Jesus did. But we are certainly called to embrace the objective that hid behind his actions—to encourage faith in Seekers (and Disciples alike). We are called to be nurturers of infant faith in those who are searching for the true purpose of their lives.

But how can we do this—especially if we aren't called to start a healing ministry and we don't perform miracles as a part of our daily routine? I'm sure there are many ways, but here are three to get you started:

1. By modeling a life of faith. "In the same way, let your light shine before men, that they may see your good deeds and praise your Father in heaven" (Matthew 5:16).

2. By speaking about your faith. "Be wise in the way you act toward outsiders; make the most of every opportunity. Let your conversation be always full of grace, seasoned with salt, so that you may know how to answer everyone" (Colossians 4:5-6).

3. By serving Seekers and Disciples. "Though I am free and belong to no man, I make myself a slave to everyone, to win as many as possible" (1 Corinthians 9:19).

There's a story about a young boy who returned home after his first Sunday school class. His mother asked, "Who was your teacher?" And the little boy replied, "I don't remember her name, but she must have been Jesus' great-grandmother because she didn't talk about anyone else."

I pray that all of us would consistently display such inspiring faith around the Seekers whom God sends our way.

- **Objective 2: To challenge people to think.**

As we've already said, people don't stop being Seekers once they become Disciples. If anything, our passion to seek out truth intensifies once we become Christians. We want to live out our faith in Christ honestly and with integrity. We want to have the freedom to think through the challenges to our beliefs that come our way. We need to be able to analyze them, openly discuss them, and search the Scriptures for real-life answers. We need to know with certainty that Christianity is built on a rock-solid foundation that will not be shaken regardless of what the world may throw at it.

Seekers also need this basic freedom—to express various ideas and think through beliefs that attempt to oppose or negate biblical truths. And even though the church is the perfect place for honest explorations like these, too often such open thinking is not only discouraged, but totally forbidden.

Thom and Joani Schultz have observed, "Some church leaders aren't altogether sure they want their people to think. They figure they've already done the thinking for their people. All their followers need to do is obey them. Without question."[17]

It's a sad truth that many of our Sunday schools and church education programs are not designed to educate at all—that is, they aren't designed to inspire people to think on their own, launch into meaningful debate with others, or openly question those in authority. No, most church programs are designed to indoctrinate. These "educational" systems don't ask questions; they give answers. To all students who attend, from youngest to oldest, their message is clear: *This is what we believe. If you believe this, too, you're welcome here! If you don't believe this, go somewhere else.*

Jesus' teaching provoked controversy. He started arguments—on purpose! His lessons inspired people to think for themselves.

But thinking is dangerous, you say! If everyone thought whatever he or she wanted to think, how would we ever arrive together at the truth?

It's quite true to say that thinking is dangerous, especially for a Seeker or a young Christian who may not have the benefit or

> *"Jesus knew that a superficial decision meant nothing. If a person wasn't going to wholeheartedly commit, there was no use in messing with him."*
>
> —Paul Woods

experience of our years of faith to guide him or her. And it may also be true that if people are allowed to think freely and disagree on the most fundamental issues of faith, then some will certainly come to the wrong conclusion about life altogether. But before we shut down that off-the-wall statement or that offensive question, consider this: If the teacher refuses to allow students to think on their own about the questions of faith, then, in the end, whose faith will they have? Their own or the teacher's? And then where will they be once the teacher is gone?

Richard C. Halverson once said:

> You may treat ideas as bullets...or seeds! You may shoot ideas...or you may sow them! You may hit people in the head with them, or you may plant them in their hearts. Use them as bullets, they kill inspiration and neutralize motivation. Use them as seeds, they take root, grow, and become a reality in the life in which they are planted. The only risk taken when seeds are planted is that they become a part of the one in whom they grow. The originator will probably get no credit for the idea.[18]

Jesus planted seeds in people's hearts. Those seeds inspired thinking and took on a life of their own within the lives of the people who heard him teach. In Mark 4:1-20, Jesus tells the famous parable of the Sower and the Seed. In that parable, Jesus describes his teaching as "seeds" and identifies four types of "soil" or people who hear him. There is one type of person who doesn't really hear the teaching at all (the hard soil). There's another who hears it and likes it, but is too shallow to incorporate it into his or her life (the shallow soil). There's also a third student who hears the teaching, likes the teaching, but is too worried about other things to really do anything with it (the choked soil). And finally, there's the good soil, the teachable student who hears the teaching, churns it over, allows it to take root, nurtures it, and eventually comes to see it produce fruit in his or her life.

Now I know most of us are very familiar with that parable, but I reviewed it because, from a teaching perspective, it makes an important point. We'll call that point Principle 3.

Principle 3
Believe that if they are teachable, they will learn.

In some ways, this principle is simply a reshaping of Principle 1 (Realize that people cannot understand truth unless God enables them). But whereas the first principle focuses on those students who cannot learn because their hearts are prideful and unyielding, this principle turns the lens the other way around and focuses on those students whose hearts are humble and seeking. Another way to put it would be to say, "Teachable students *will* learn, no matter what." A young person who is bent on learning is going to learn something regardless of the quality of your teaching, and there's really nothing you can do to stop it. All that you can do—and what you must do—is help shape *what* those students learn, guiding them to think on their own in such a way that true learning occurs.

Thom and Joani Schultz sum it up nicely when they write: "Learning is a consequence of thinking. If our people aren't thinking, they're not growing in their faith."[19]

I think Jesus would agree.

• **Objective 3: To provoke to decision.**

Christians have never been called to timidity. And for teachers, that call to courage is doubly true—for we are not only called to follow Christ courageously in our own lives, but also to inspire and support that same courageous faith in others. As teachers following the Master, we must present the truth of God's message as clearly and compellingly as our words and lifestyle will permit. Failing to do this will inevitably result in giving in to what Annie Dillard calls "the enormous temptation in all of life to diddle around making itsy-bitsy friends and meals and journeys for itsy-bitsy years on end."[20] The truth that Jesus taught, however, was far more real and requires far more courage to lay out plainly for people to see. Says Dillard: "The world is wider than that in all directions, more dangerous and more bitter, more extravagant and bright. We are...raising tomatoes when we should be raising Cain, or Lazarus."[21]

Jesus' teaching provoked people to decision. People could not walk away from an encounter with Jesus unprovoked. His words and actions moved the people he encountered. Some were moved toward Christ; others were moved away. But all were moved.

In John 3:1-21, the Apostle John records just such a "moving" encounter between Jesus and Nicodemus. Listen to just a few of the Teacher's words as he lovingly provoked Nicodemus toward a point of decision.

"I tell you the truth, no one can see the kingdom of God unless he is born again" (John 3:3).

"I have spoken to you of earthly things and you do not believe; how then will you believe if I speak of heavenly things?" (John 3:12).

"For God so loved the world that he gave his one and only Son, that whoever believes in him shall not perish but have eternal life" (John 3:16).

"But whoever lives by the truth comes into the light, so that it may be seen plainly that what he has done has been done through God" (John 3:21).

Of course, we never want to alienate Seekers or Disciples unnecessarily by what we say or do. But as teachers who want to teach the way Jesus taught, when the time is right, we must not shrink back from the goal of provoking people to decision. Just as Jesus did with Nicodemus—and, most likely, with each of us as well.

Teacher's Corner:
A Word About Labeling Seekers and Opponents

Separating students into labeled categories can be helpful when it allows us to tie together similarities and themes in the personalities and attitudes of the people we teach. But labels are dangerous too—especially if we treat them as rigid definitions. Dan Allender, co-author of *Bold Love,* offers this advice:

> A rigid definition implies that I am what I am and will always be that in the future. But the heart and soul of a person are not eternally enslaved to a particular direction or to certain symptoms. Change can occur to a point where it can be said of the thief, the gossip, or the adulterer, "That is what some of you were" (1 Corinthians 6:11). Sufficient change can occur that invalidates the label. For that reason, I am never to judge you. I may assess your current condition and offer a tentative hypothesis, "You appear to be a fool," but I am never to say, "You are and will always be a fool." That statement is the dictum of a judge who has passed a final, unchangeable verdict. It is imperative never to feel certain or resolute about our opinion. We must remain open to seeing the facts from a new perspective and equally open to the possibility that our perception is distorted by the log in our own eye.[22]

As teachers we have great power to impact our students' sense of identity and self-worth. We must carefully follow the Holy Spirit and God's Word in discerning which of our students has a seeking heart and which has an unbelieving heart. We should always use discernment with caution and hold our labels loosely. Our assessment of what is must never become a judgment of what must be. God is bigger than our labels.

Objective for Opponents

Before I state Jesus' objective for his opponents, let me remind you that by "opponent" I do not mean what many evangelicals now call "pre-Christians." That is, I am not referring to people who have even the slightest desire within them to pursue, accept, or believe the claims of Christ or Christianity. By "opponent," I mean one who has not only rejected Christianity, but who also undermines its progress in other people's lives—often intentionally.

That is not to say that an "opponent" has no hope of becoming a Christian. At one point in his life, the Apostle Paul would have easily been considered an "opponent" in the sense I just described. But he experienced a turning point that set his life on the right course. While he was still an opponent, however, his attitude was hostile toward Christianity, and his heart was unyielding, stubborn, and unteachable. It is that unteachable heart that defines the opponent. And whenever Jesus encountered someone with a heart like that, he had only one goal:

- **To expose hypocrisy, pride, and unbelief.**

Now there isn't a Christian, living or dead, who hasn't struggled with all three of these sins at some point. But in an unbelieving heart, these sins often become so ingrained that the only hope for change is radical—and sometimes public—exposure. Far from vindictive or cruel, such a bold act of confrontation can be the epitome of "tough love." When people become so hardened and unaware of their own sin, sometimes the only way to open their eyes is to draw open the shades and make them see it plainly—often by letting them see themselves through others' eyes.

It's a calculated, planned disruption of an opponent's life, and it's one of the hardest things for a teacher to do. But sometimes it's the only thing left to do.

When I was around ten years old, my family lived in a small east

Texas town where my father pastored the town's largest church. As the immature son of a pastor, I was cocky, irreverent, and believed I had the divine right to do whatever I pleased, whenever I wished—especially at church, where I spent most of my time. To most of my teachers, I was simply a brat—unteachable, unyielding, and unbelieving.

On a particular Sunday morning at Sunday school, my teacher, Mr. Eckman, brought with him a young boy who lived in his neighborhood. I don't even remember his name. But he was shy, and awkward, and not sure what to say—in short, a perfect target. For that entire hour as Mr. Eckman tried to teach the lesson, I poked and joked and sneered and made fun of the awkward boy. I got others to join in too. Whispers abounded, followed again and again by snorts and hushed laughter. The boy never responded, but only pretended to listen to Mr. Eckman or stared absently at his shoes.

Mr. Eckman ended class early, which I didn't expect. Then he did something else I didn't expect. He asked his guest to step outside and wait for him. Once the boy was gone, Mr. Eckman pointed directly at me (the pastor's son!) and said, "In one hour, you have probably ruined a relationship that has taken me months to build. This was his first time to ever set foot in a church, and I now doubt he will ever do it again. I hope that you understand how selfish and cruel you have been today." With that, he quietly walked out.

I never spoke to Mr. Eckman about that incident again. But I remember his words today as clearly as if he'd just spoken them. I had never felt so exposed or embarrassed in my young life. That day, for the first time that I can remember, I prayed earnestly for someone other than myself. I prayed for that boy. And I repented for what I had done. But I never would have unless my teacher had been willing to expose my sin.

If you'd like to examine this "tough love" aspect of teaching further, check out these examples drawn from Christ's ministry:

- Luke 11:29-32 (Jesus rebukes an unbelieving generation).
- Luke 11:37–12:3 (Jesus proclaims "six woes" against the hypocritical Pharisees).
- Matthew 11:20-24 (Jesus denounces unrepentant cities).
- Mark 10:17-22 (Jesus exposes the materialistic pride of the rich, young ruler).
- Acts 9:1-16 (Jesus confronts Saul's wrong behavior).

Methods of the Master

Now for a quick review of Jesus' teaching goal and objectives. I'd suggest you commit these to memory.

Jesus' Goal (Principle 2)

The ultimate goal of Christian teaching is to draw people into a genuine, personal relationship with God.

Jesus' Objective for Disciples

1. To build relationships.
2. To train in love.
3. To train in faith and obedience.
4. To send in boldness.

Jesus' Objectives for Seekers (and Disciples)

1. To encourage in faith.
2. To challenge people to think.
3. To provoke to decision.

Jesus' Objective to Opponents

1. To expose hypocrisy, pride, and unbelief.

Now that we know the "why" behind Jesus' teaching, how do we apply it? The next six chapters are dedicated to helping us begin to answer that question. We'll look in depth at several of the methods Jesus used to accomplish his goal and objectives, and we'll examine how we can apply those same methods to our teaching today.

Some of the methods we'll encounter in the pages ahead may seem unusual and even absurd. But that shouldn't surprise us much—God's ways have always appeared at times to be illogical, unreasonable, or silly. Charles Stanley writes:

> Jesus usually did the opposite of what people expected. If we feel the tug of the world and what we hear from God seems reasonable and rational, then we should check it out. That's not to say that God doesn't utilize human wisdom. He does. But on many occasions God's Voice will ask us to accomplish something that seems quite illogical to our rational minds.[23]

It should be no wonder to us, then, if some of the methods Jesus used in his teaching should seem odd or illogical to us. But as we'll see, every technique he applied had eternal results in the lives of the people he taught. As we learn to teach as he taught, we, too, can see eternal results.

[1] Gene Edwards, *The Secret to the Christian Life,* Vol.2 (Auburn, ME: The Seed Sowers, 1991), 1-2.

[2] Thom and Joani Schultz, *Why Nobody Learns Much of Anything at Church: And How to Fix It* (Loveland, CO: Group Publishing, 1993), 20.

[3] Michael Collins, *Carrying the Fire* (New York, NY: Farrar, Straus, and Giroux, 1974), 469-471.

[4] *The Teaching Ministry of the Church,* ed. by Daryl Eldridge (Nashville, TN: Broadman & Holman, 1995), 40, as quoted in *Teaching as Jesus Taught.*

[5] Michael D. Warden, *Small-Group Body Builders* (Loveland, CO: Group Publishing, 1998), 98.

[6] Vine's Expository Dictionary of Biblical Words, ed. by W.E. Vine, Merrill F. Unger, and William White, Jr. (Nashville, TN: Thomas Nelson Publishers, 1985), 346.

[7] Vine's Expository Dictionary of Biblical Words, 531.

[8] Schultz, *Why Nobody Learns Much of Anything at Church: And How to Fix It,* 28.

[9] Dick Gruber, "Heart Matters: Lance, Leader of Men," Children's Ministry Magazine (May/June 1996), 62.

[10] For more information on the lives of these men after Pentecost, see *Foxe's Book of Martyrs* by John Foxe, 6-7, 12-13.

[11] Time span between Paul's exposure to Christ's teaching and his subsequent conversion is based on the "New Testament Time Line" in the Disciple's Study Bible (Nashville, TN: Holman Bible Publishers, 1988), 1186.

[12] Sister Regina M. Alfonso, *How Jesus Taught* (Staten Island, NY: Alba House, 1986), 15-34.

[13] C.S. Lewis, *Thē Four Loves,* quoted by Dr. Dan B. Allender and Dr. Tremper Longman III, *Bold Love* (Colorado Springs, CO: NavPress, 1992).

[14] Allender and Longman, *Bold Love,* 32.

[15] Quote by Ambrose Bierce in *Illustrations Unlimited,* ed. by James S. Hewett, (Wheaton, IL: Tyndale House Publishers, 1988), 187. Used by permission of Tyndale House Publishers, Inc. All rights reserved.

[16] Story adapted from *Illustrations Unlimited,* ed. by James S. Hewett, 490. Used by permission of Tyndale House Publishers, Inc. All rights reserved.

[17] Schultz, *Why Nobody Learns Much of Anything at Church: And How to Fix It,* 87.

[18] Quote by Richard C. Halverson in *Illustrations Unlimited,* ed. by James S. Hewett, 481. Used by permission of Tyndale House Publishers, Inc. All rights reserved.

[19] Schultz, *Why Nobody Learns Much of Anything at Church: And How to Fix It,* 88.

[20] Quote by Annie Dillard in *Illustrations Unlimited,* ed. by James S. Hewett, 492. Used by permission of Tyndale House Publishers, Inc. All rights reserved.

[21] Ibid.

[22] Allender and Longman, *Bold Love,* 232.

[23] Charles Stanley, *How to Listen to God* (Nashville, TN: Thomas Nelson, Inc., 1985), 52.

Chapter 4
Using Sayings and Parables

"The disciples came to him and asked,
'Why do you speak to the people in parables?'
He replied, 'The knowledge of the secrets of the kingdom
of heaven has been given to you, but not to them.
Whoever has will be given more, and he will have an abundance.
Whoever does not have, even what he has will be taken from him.
This is why I speak to them in parables:
Though seeing, they do not see; though hearing,
they do not hear or understand.
But blessed are your eyes because they see,
and your ears because they hear.' "
—Matthew 13:10-13, 16

Remember *Life's Little Instruction Book*? It's a compact volume of wisdom "nuggets" by H. Jackson Brown Jr., which he originally created for his son as he went away to college. Upon its release, the little book immediately made a big impact on popular culture. It seemed like nearly everyone bought a copy. And we all started reading these little pearls of wisdom, not just to ourselves, but to each other at the office or over coffee after dinner. So many of us were fascinated by the skillful way Brown could pack so much meaning into so few words.

The demand for Brown's pearls of wisdom became so great, in fact, that two more volumes of the little book were published, just as quickly as Brown could churn them out. To date, he has written no less than 1,560 tidbits of wisdom for us to consume.

Here are some of my favorites:

"Don't live with the brakes on."[1]

"Remember that great love and great achievements involve great risk."[2]

"Remember that life's most treasured moments often come

unannounced."[3]

"Never say anything uncomplimentary about another person's dog."[4]

Pithy statements about life are nothing new. In fact, if we stopped to think about it, most of us could think of a few axioms we've heard at some time in the past that have gone on to shape the way we live and see the world around us. Most are so common as to be considered cliché by many—but they still have a way of seeping into the way we think about life. For example:

"What goes around comes around."

"You get what you pay for."

"The proof is in the pudding."

"You can never go home again."

"Waste not, want not."

"All's well that ends well."

"The early bird gets the worm."

Even though we may not "believe everything we hear" concerning sayings like these, we still never forget them. Something has etched them into our memories. And, to some degree at least, they affect the way we think, make decisions, and process our experiences in life.

This is starting to sound like a wonderful teaching tool, isn't it? Well, it is!

How Jesus Made the Truth Unforgettable

People may call them proverbs, wise sayings, maxims, adages, sage advice, or rules for living, but most aphorisms like those we mentioned earlier actually do have technical names. In fact, there are more than a dozen different types of pithy statements that can be used to help people remember what you're teaching. And Jesus used them all, in a variety of ways.

Here's a quick list of the most common types of maxims Jesus used. We'll explain these further as we explore how we can use these tools in our own teaching.

Contrast—A maxim that contrasts one thing with another. "Do not store up for yourselves treasures on earth, where moth and rust destroy, and where thieves break in and steal. But store up for yourselves treasures in heaven, where moth and rust do not destroy, and where thieves do not break in and steal" (Matthew 6:19-20).

Enigma—A maxim that is purposefully vague or obscure, in order to challenge students to think. "Wherever there is a carcass, there the vultures will gather" (Matthew 24:28).

Humor—A maxim that presents a truth in a way that seems ludicrous or unexpected. "Again I tell you, it is easier for a camel to go through the eye of a needle than for a rich man to enter the kingdom of God" (Matthew 19:24).

Hyperbole—A maxim that uses exaggeration to emphasize a truth or principle. "If your right eye causes you to sin, gouge it out and throw it away. It is better for you to lose one part of your body than for your whole body to be thrown into hell" (Matthew 5:29).

Hypocatastasis—A maxim that renames a person or thing in order to describe or emphasize it's inherent qualities. "Be on your guard against the yeast of the Pharisees and Sadducees" (Matthew 16:6b).

Metaphor—A maxim that compares two people or things by directly equating them. "You are the light of the world" (Matthew 5:14a).

Metonymy—A maxim that uses symbolic language to describe or explain a truth. "A city on a hill cannot be hidden" (Matthew 5:14b).

Paradox—A maxim that appears to sound contradictory, but really isn't. "Whoever finds his life will lose it, and whoever loses his life for my sake will find it" (Matthew 10:39).

Personification—A maxim that ascribes human characteristics to things that aren't human. "The wind blows wherever it pleases. You hear its sound, but you cannot tell where it comes from or where it is going. So it is with everyone born of the Spirit" (John 3:8).

Pun—A maxim that contains similar-sounding words with different meanings, or the same word with two meanings. "I tell you the truth, no one can see the kingdom of God unless he is born again" (John 3:3). The Greek word *anōthen* is translated as "again" in this verse, but it also means "from above." Thus, Jesus' statement had a double meaning.[5]

Simile—A maxim that compares two people or things by using "like" or "as." "Again he said, 'What shall we say the kingdom of God is like, or what parable shall we use to describe it? It is like a mustard seed, which is the smallest seed you plant in the ground. Yet when planted, it grows and becomes the largest of all garden plants, with such big branches that the birds of the air can perch in its shade'" (Mark 4:30-32).

For all the variety of maxim types listed above, they can all be summed up in a single, simple definition:

"A maxim is a truth wrapped in a saying."

That's a little different than saying a maxim is simply a "statement of truth." Let me explain what I mean. A "statement of truth" might be to say that "a person's character can be determined by looking at the way he or she lives." True enough, but that's not nearly as memorable as Jesus' maxim: "A tree is recognized by its fruit" (Matthew 12:33b). Maxims are creative and specifically designed not only to be truthful, but also to be memorable.

What follows is a partial listing of Jesus' maxims in the Gospels. As you read through them, note how easy it would be for you to remember each one. And just for fun, see if you can identify which type of maxim Jesus is using in each statement.

"You are the salt of the earth."	Matthew 5:13
"You are the light of the world."	Matthew 5:14
"A city on a hill cannot be hidden."	Matthew 5:14
"For where your treasure is, there your heart will be also."	Matthew 6:21; Luke 12:34
"The eye is the lamp of the body."	Matthew 6:22; Luke 11:34
"No one can serve two masters."	Matthew 6:24
"With the measure you use, it will be measured to you."	Matthew 7:2; Mark 4:24; Luke 6:38
"A good tree cannot bear bad fruit, and a bad tree cannot bear good fruit."	Matthew 7:18; Luke 6:43
"A student is not above his teacher, nor a servant above his master."	Matthew 10:24; Luke 6:40; John 13:16; 15:20
"Whoever finds his life will lose it, and whoever loses his life for my sake will find it."	Matthew 10:39; 16:25; Mark 8:35; Luke 9:24; 17:33; John 12:25
"Wisdom is proved right by her actions."	Matthew 11:19
"Every kingdom divided against itself will be ruined, and every city or household divided against itself will not stand."	Matthew 12:25; Mark 3:25; Luke 11:17
"A tree is recognized by its fruit."	Matthew 12:33; Luke 6:44
"Out of the overflow of the heart the mouth speaks."	Matthew 12:34; Luke 6:45

"If a blind man leads a blind man, both will fall into a pit."	Matthew 15:14; Luke 6:39
"Many who are first will be last, and many who are last will be first."	Matthew 19:30; Mark 10:31
"Whoever wants to become great among you must be your servant, and whoever wants to be first must be your slave."	Matthew 20:26-27; Mark 10:43-44; Luke 22:26
"For many are invited, but few are chosen."	Matthew 22:14
"For whoever exalts himself will be humbled, and whoever humbles himself will be exalted."	Matthew 23:12; Luke 14:11; 18:14
"All who draw the sword will die by the sword."	Matthew 26:52

Jesus used maxims like these in his teaching for a variety of reasons. For example, Jesus used maxims to

• help people understand the truth (by using contrast or symbolism, such as in Luke 6:43);

• cause people to remember the truth (through humor, pun, or other techniques, such as in Mark 10:25); and

• challenge people to examine the truth more deeply (by creating an enigma or paradox, such as in Matthew 19:30).

It's easy to see why Jesus used maxims so often instead of teaching with simple "statements of truth." Maxims are fun. They're intriguing. And they have of way of sticking with you whether you want to remember them or not. As William Barclay writes in his book *The Mind of Jesus:*

> Such sayings have the gadfly of truth in them. Their supreme quality is that they will not leave a man alone. He cannot forget them. Every now and then they flash unbidden into his mind. Even when he would willingly forget them, they flash across the screen of his memory and leave him thinking and wondering. Often Jesus taught in sayings which refuse to be forgotten.[6]

Sounds like a great technique for us to develop as teachers who want to follow in Jesus' steps, doesn't it? In fact, it's one of the foundational tools of Jesus' teaching and a powerful principle for us to follow.

Principle 4
Maximize your maxims.

Maxims are easy tools that we can use with students right away. And the best part is that most of the maxims we would ever need have already been created—we just have to look them up! Two of the three best sources for maxims are found in the Bible. One, of course, is the Gospels. Jesus used maxims more than any other New Testament teacher, and most (if not all) of his pithy sayings can be found in the pages of the Gospels. The second source is in the Old Testament book of Proverbs and, to a lesser degree, Ecclesiastes. These books contain the sayings of Solomon and other wise men of Israel. One other great source for maxims can be found at your local library under the topic "famous quotes." There's a wide array of "quotable quote" books out there, and many of them contain gems of wisdom and insight that you can use to package the truth in memorable, challenging statements.

As powerful as maxims are in helping people learn more effectively, there is another method that Jesus often used in conjunction with maxims to help people learn and remember the truth—the parable. Let's take a look at this well-known but little-understood teaching method to see how we can incorporate it into our teaching today.

Packaging the Truth in Parables

We've already stated that a maxim is simply "a truth wrapped in a saying." A parable can be described just as simply:

"A parable is a truth wrapped in a story."

Stories make up the fabric of life. Through them we learn, we understand each other and our world, and they often lead us to change and grow. Perhaps that's why God sent Jesus—to tell us a story about God's salvation, composed in flesh and blood. And perhaps that's why Jesus used parables—stories—to explain, illustrate, or illuminate the truths that he wanted people to know.

"If it can be totally grasped and understood, it's probably not a parable. There's always something more there. There's that next layer, and there's more to be revealed and thought through."

—Bill Korte

But if Jesus used parables to help people understand the truth more clearly, why did he make this perplexing statement in Matthew 13:10-13?

"The disciples came to him and asked, 'Why do you speak to the people in parables?'

He replied, 'The knowledge of the secrets of the kingdom of heaven has been given to you, but not to them. Whoever has will be given more, and he will have an abundance. Whoever does not have, even what he has will be taken from him. This is why I speak to them in parables: Though seeing, they do not see; though hearing, they do not hear or understand.' "

Perhaps the answer can be found in looking back at the type of maxim called an enigma. An enigma is a maxim that is purposefully vague or obscure in order to challenge the listener to think. For example, here are a few enigmas that Jesus used in his teaching:

"Whoever eats my flesh and drinks my blood remains in me, and I in him" (John 6:56).

"Let the dead bury their own dead" (Matthew 8:22b).

"Many who are first will be last, and many who are last will be first" (Matthew 19:30).

Teacher's Corner: Humility and Openness Required

Remember Principle 1? "People cannot understand truth unless God enables them." Enigmas and parables only work with students who are humble and open to learning.

Can you see how enigmas like these cause the listener to stop and think? Such statements cannot be understood unless the listener is willing to pause and process the statement until it makes sense. It requires effort and a teachable attitude.

Parables are similar to enigmas because they, too, require people to think and examine the truth for themselves. Not all who listened to Jesus' parables understood the truths he was trying to convey—not because the parables were too difficult to understand, but because their hearts were not willing to learn. When Jesus made his startling statement in Matthew 13:10-13, he was probably referring to people like that—people with unteachable hearts.

I've seen many Christian educators who

"There's a real reluctance among Christians to take that risk and do what Jesus did by telling a story and putting the responsibility on the people to discover what the truth is."

—Rick Lawrence

believe it is necessary to spoon-feed the truth of the Bible to their students. They lay out the truth before people in a way that requires absolutely no effort at all from the learners. They need only sit there with their mouths open while the teacher pours the truth in and sometimes even helps them chew and swallow it. Although on the surface this may seem to be the most loving and effective way of conveying God's truth to others, such a method fails to recognize a fundamental truth about human nature. I'll phrase it as a maxim to help you remember:

"A parable as a story can be understood even by the youngest. Because what do children ask for? A story. And that's something children continue to ask as they become teenagers and young adults. 'Will you tell a story?' And if those stories are actually parables, then they can grow through storytelling all through their lives."

—Bill Korte

A truth told is easily forgotten,
but a truth discovered lasts a lifetime.

Parables do not *tell;* they *show.* And in the showing, they inspire people to think about the meaning behind the story and discover the truth for themselves. It can feel like a risky way of teaching, because there will always be some students who hear the parable and fail to immediately grasp its meaning. *But that kind of risk is a necessary aspect of effective teaching*—especially for those of us who want to teach the way Jesus taught.

Consider these insightful thoughts from William Barclay in *The Mind of Jesus:*

> Truth can never be inserted into a man like a pill or an injection; truth is like a goal to which a man's mind under the guidance and the stimulus of God must journey in its own seeking.
>
> The great value of the parable is that it does not impose truth on a man; it puts a man in a position in which he can go on to discover, or to realize, truth for himself.[7]

Remember Principle 3? "Believe that if they are teachable, they *will* learn." Parables don't force truths on people. Instead, they set out a story that must be unwrapped for the truth within it to be seen. There will always be some who will refuse to unwrap the story on their own, and, sadly, they will miss the point. But in time, and with God's help, any student with a teachable heart will eventually unwrap the story and understand it. And when they do, the lessons they learn will stay with them for a lifetime.

The Parables of Jesus[8]

Parable	Reference
Lamp on a lamp stand	Matthew 5:14-15; Mark 4:21-22; Luke 8:16-17; 11:33
Building on rock or sand	Matthew 7:24-27; Luke 6:47-49
New patch on old garment	Matthew 9:16; Mark 2:21; Luke 5:36
New wine in old wineskins	Matthew 9:17; Mark 2:22; Luke 5:37-38
Sower and the seed	Matthew 13:3-8, 18-23; Mark 4:3-8, 14-20; Luke 8:5-8, 11-15
Wheat and weeds	Matthew 13:24-30, 36-43
Mustard seed	Matthew 13:31-32; Mark 4:30-32; Luke 13:18-19
Yeast in bread	Matthew 13:33; Luke 13:20-21
Hidden treasure	Matthew 13:44
Pearl of great price	Matthew 13:45-46
Fishing net	Matthew 13:47-50
Head of household	Matthew 13:52
Lost sheep	Matthew 18:12-14; Luke 15:4-7
Unmerciful servant	Matthew 18:23-34
Workers in the vineyard	Matthew 20:1-16
Two sons	Matthew 21:28-32
Tenants	Matthew 21:33-44; Mark 12:1-11; Luke 20:9-18
Marriage of the king's son	Matthew 22:2-14
Fig tree	Matthew 24:32-33; Mark 13:28-29; Luke 21:29-31
Faithful and wise servant	Matthew 24:45-51; Luke 12:42-48
Ten virgins	Matthew 25:1-13
Talents	Matthew 25:14-30; Luke 19:12-27
Sheep and goats	Matthew 25:31-46
Growing seed	Mark 4:26-29
Watchful servants	Mark 13:35-37; Luke 12:35-40
Two debtors	Luke 7:41-43

Good Samaritan	Luke 10:30-37
Persistent friend	Luke 11:5-8
Rich fool	Luke 12:16-21
Barren fig tree	Luke 13:6-9
Low seat at the feast	Luke 14:7-14
Great banquet	Luke 14:16-24
Tower	Luke 14:28-30
King at war	Luke 14:31-32
Lost coin	Luke 15:8-10
Prodigal son	Luke 15:11-32
Shrewd manager	Luke 16:1-8
Rich man and Lazarus	Luke 16:19-31
Master and servant	Luke 17:7-10
Unjust judge	Luke 18:2-8
Pharisee and the tax collector	Luke 18:10-14

Bringing Parables and Maxims Together

Although Jesus used parables and sayings separately, he also used them together quite often—by following a parable with a maxim that somehow illustrated or explained it. Here's a list of parables in which Jesus also used a maxim. Pick a few to read through, so you can see how using maxims and parables together can make both teaching methods more effective:

Parable	Reference
Workers in the vineyard	Matthew 20:1-16
Tenants	Matthew 21:33-44
Marriage of the king's son	Matthew 22:2-14
Fig tree	Matthew 24:32-35
Talents	Matthew 25:14-30
Sheep and goats	Matthew 25:31-46
Two debtors	Luke 7:41-47
Persistent friend	Luke 11:5-10
Rich fool	Luke 12:16-23
Low seat at the feast	Luke 14:7-14

Great banquet	Luke 14:16-47
King at war	Luke 14:31-32
Shrewd manager	Luke 16:1-10
Pharisee and tax collector	Luke 18:10-14

Even in this brief overview, we can see how using parables and maxims can be effective as teaching tools. But aren't there other effective teaching tools, too? What about lecturing, using questions, and creating learning experiences? (We'll discuss each of these methods in later chapters, by the way). With so many other teaching methods available, why did Jesus use parables and maxims so often? There are at least four important reasons:

1. Parables and maxims are memorable. George Vasallo, a writer for USA Today, recently interviewed John McDonald, who has authored at least seventy best-selling novels. One of the questions Vasallo asked the novelist was, "What's the best advice you've ever been given?"

McDonald replied, "Don't tell 'em, show 'em." Then he went on to explain the "bad version: Fred was a man with a very bad case of body odor.

"Better version: As Fred came walking down the country road, a herd of goats looked at him in consternation, then all ran off into a field gagging and coughing."[9]

Which version of McDonald's example is more memorable? The second one, of course! Who can forget the image of a herd of goats running madly away from a smelly

"Forget facts and figures. In fact, that's what people do—they forget facts and figures, but they remember stories. So whenever you can, tell a story because that's what people will remember long-term."

—Thom Schultz

man, gagging and coughing as they go? And did you notice the maxim McDonald used? "Don't tell 'em, show 'em."

Few people in the world would argue that the greatest influence on the world's cultures in the last twenty-five years hasn't come from mighty military campaigns or persuasive political speeches. It has come from Hollywood. Through their exported movies, TV shows, advertisements, and music, American storytellers are influencing people's lives all over the world. Hollywood tells stories better than anyone, and the effects are astounding.

Unfortunately, this renaissance of storytelling has rarely reached into the church. In fact, most of us have shunned the most powerful story-tellers of our time because we don't like the ungodly story lines they create or the filthy language their movies contain. Although our convictions are admirable, I believe we are inadvertently missing out on what is perhaps the most powerful movement of our times. Stories have the power to change lives like few things can. And in our culture, the greatest storytellers are not Christians, but creative men and women like Spielberg, Katzenberg, Geffen, Crichton and Steel. These are ordinary people who have become masters at "showing" instead of "telling." And, unfortunately, they could be impacting the world more than the church.

The principle of "show, don't tell" doesn't apply only to best-selling authors like McDonald or Steel, or movie-makers like Spielberg. It also applies to Christian teachers—like you and me—who want to make the truths we present unforgettable.

Of course, most of us don't have the opportunity to publish a best-selling novel or create a blockbuster movie. But then, neither did Jesus. Through his skillful use of parables and maxims, Jesus made the truth of God unforgettable, and so impacted his generation that he was able to change the course of history. And, with God's help, so can we.

2. Parables and maxims inspire thinking. Parables carry the intrigue of an illustration or analogy. The stories Jesus presented in his teaching carried a meaning hidden just below the surface. It's like a kind of puzzle that the hearer naturally wants to solve. Who wouldn't be intrigued by a statement like this?

"The kingdom of heaven is like treasure hidden in a field. When a man found it, he hid it again, and then in his joy went and sold all he had and bought that field" (Matthew 13:44).

Why did the man who found the treasure hide it again? Why did he buy the field and not simply take the treasure? What sort of treasure would cause him to joyfully sell everything he had?

Even a simple parable like this can inspire questions that take a long time to answer...because they require the listener to think. Jesus rarely spoon-fed the truth to his disciples. Instead, his use of parables invited them to grapple with questions they might not otherwise consider.

The best maxims, too, create a disequilibrium in our thinking. They have a way of throwing us off balance intellectually; challenging us to think about what's being said and apply it to our experience. Consider these examples:

"There is nothing concealed that will not be disclosed, or hidden that will not be made known" (Matthew 10:26b).

"Whoever finds his life will lose it, and whoever loses his life for my sake will find it" (Matthew 10:39).

"The last will be first, and the first will be last" (Matthew 20:16).

"What is highly valued among men is detestable in God's sight" (Luke 16:15b).

These statements have a way of unsettling our minds and provoking us to think about whether they might be true. As Barclay writes,

> The great value of these sayings is their long-term disturbing power. When a man first hears them, he may well dismiss them as fantastic and unreal and incredible and untrue. But something has been dropped into his mind which even against his will compels him to think, and, if he goes on thinking for long enough, conclusions will force themselves upon him, even if he does not wish them to be true. In many ways Jesus is the great disturber, and not least in these thought-compelling paradoxes which he dropped into the minds and hearts of men.[10]

As a master teacher, Jesus understood the value of making people think for themselves. Parables and maxims provided two powerful tools that inspired such thinking, and, as a result, led many of his listeners to a deeper and more personal understanding of the truth.

3. Parables and sayings have multiple applications. Because they focus on principles instead of specific circumstances, the truths wrapped in parables and sayings can be applied to the wide variety of situations people face.

Take, for example, the parable of the Talents in Matthew 25:14-30. As you read through the parable, look for the principle(s) Jesus is illustrating.

> Again, [the kingdom of heaven] will be like a man going on a journey, who called his servants and entrusted his property to them. To one he gave five talents of money, to another two talents, and to another one talent, each according to his ability. Then he went on his journey. The man

who had received the five talents went at once and put his money to work and gained five more. So also, the one with the two talents gained two more. But the man who had received the one talent went off, dug a hole in the ground and hid his master's money.

After a long time the master of those servants returned and settled accounts with them. The man who had received the five talents brought the other five. "Master," he said, "you entrusted me with five talents. See, I have gained five more."

His master replied, "Well done, good and faithful servant! You have been faithful with a few things; I will put you in charge of many things. Come and share your master's happiness!"

The man with the two talents also came, "Master," he said, "you entrusted me with two talents; see, I have gained two more."

His master replied, "Well done, good and faithful servant! You have been faithful with a few things; I will put you in charge of many things. Come and share your master's happiness!"

Then the man who had received the one talent came. "Master," he said, "I knew that you are a hard man, harvesting where you have not sown and gathering where you have not scattered seed. So I was afraid and went out and hid your talent in the ground. See, here is what belongs to you."

His master replied, "You wicked, lazy servant! So you knew that I harvest where I have not sown and gather where I have not scattered seed? Well then, you should have put my money on deposit with the bankers, so that when I returned I would have received it back with interest.

"Take the talent from him and give it to the one who has the ten talents. For everyone who has will be given more, and he will have an abundance. Whoever does not have, even what he has will be taken from him. And throw that worthless servant outside, into the darkness, where there will be weeping and gnashing of teeth."

What principle(s) is Jesus trying to emphasize? It's stated in the form of a maxim at the end of the parable: "For everyone who has will be given more, and he will have an abundance. Whoever does not have, even what he has will be taken from him" (Matthew 25:29).

In other words, whoever takes what he or she has been given by

God and risks investing it in order to see it grow and multiply will be blessed. But whoever ignores God's gift or refuses to risk investing it will eventually lose it completely. That's a weighty truth, isn't it?

Now, on the lines below, jot down a few ways this principle can be applied to your life. I've provided a few examples to get you started:

• Don't be afraid to risk investing the financial blessings God brings to your life.

• Make it a priority to develop and expand the talents and abilities God has given you.

• _____

_____

• _____

_____

• _____

_____

If we could compare what you have written in the spaces above with what one hundred other people wrote, we'd probably find at least one hundred different applications for the principle Jesus taught. And that's just scratching the surface.

Because parables and maxims focus on principles, they apply to everyone! And by using parables and sayings in our teaching, we allow our students to personalize the principles we teach and apply them practically to their own lives.

4. Parables and sayings work effectively with all types of listeners. Remember the categories for the types of people Jesus dealt with?

Disciples—Those who have committed their lives to following Christ.

Seekers—Those who are teachable, but have not yet made a commitment to follow Christ.

Opponents—Those who reject Christ's message and influence others to do the same, purposefully or not.

Jesus' parables and sayings had a powerful effect on each type of listener he encountered. For his disciples and those seekers around him, his parables and maxims provided a powerful source of learning and amazement. But for unbelievers such as the Pharisees, Jesus' teachings usually produced antagonism, often because the parables and maxims were targeted directly at their sinful practices. As an example, notice the difference in reactions between the Pharisees and the crowd in Matthew 21:45-46, just after Jesus told the parable of the Tenants: "When the chief priests and the Pharisees heard Jesus' parables, they knew he was talking about them. They looked for a way to arrest him, but they were afraid of the crowd because the people held that he was a prophet."

Now we might be tempted to think that parables and maxims are useless when dealing with resistant or unteachable students. But that was not Jesus' attitude. In fact, when his disciples asked him why he taught in parables, he said it was *because* of those people whose hearts are hard.

"The disciples came to him and asked, 'Why do you speak to the people in parables?' He replied, 'The knowledge of the secrets of the kingdom of heaven has been given to you, but not to them. Whoever has will be given more, and he will have an abundance. Whoever does not have, even what he has will be taken from him. This is why I speak to them in parables: Though seeing, they do not see; though hearing, they do not hear or understand' " (Matthew 13:10-13).

Teaching with parables exposes people whose hearts are hard and unyielding, primarily because understanding and accepting the meaning of a parable requires a humble and teachable spirit. People with unteachable hearts refuse to humble themselves and process a parable's meaning. And so the meaning is lost to them. Jesus used parables and maxims to prevent cheapening the truth by tossing it out freely before those who would not appreciate or respect it. As Roy Zuck states:

> Like soil unresponsive to seed, their calloused hearts prevented their receiving certain truths given in parables. "The knowledge of the secrets of the kingdom of heaven has been given to you, *but not to them*" (Matthew 13:11, author emphasis)...Therefore because their minds were closed to the King and his kingdom, the meaning of the parables of the secrets of the kingdom were closed to them too. By concealing the truth from those hardened to it, Jesus was following his own advice not to give what is holy to dogs or pearls to pigs (Matthew 7:6).[11]

As we stated earlier, as Christian teachers it is not our job to decide who among our students is teachable and who is not. At the same time, however, it *is* our job to present God's truth in way that is honorable and does not cheapen its value by throwing it out to those who would only trample it underfoot. Parables and maxims provide us with a powerful tool for teaching as Jesus taught, in a way that honors the truth and produces a permanent impact on those who learn.

Now let's explore how we can create and use parables and maxims in our teaching today.

Modern-Day Stories and Maxims

If you can tell a story, you can use parables and maxims in your teaching just as Jesus did. It's easy!

We've already mentioned a few places where you can find tons of maxims, adages, and sayings to use in your teaching. Here are a few more:

• The Internet—Search for the appropriate Web sites using words such as "quotes," "Christian," "religious," and "famous."

• Your pastor—He or she probably has many books of illustrations and quotable quotes.

• Your own experiences—In your years on earth, you've probably come up with a few truth-packed gems of your own. Don't be afraid to use them!

Finding sources for parables and parable creation can be just as easy. Parables are all around you, every day. You just have to watch for them. Here are just a few great sources where you can find parables or the inspiration for creating parables of your own:

• Movies—People always talk about the latest movie to hit the screens, so why not use that common experience as a source for parables? Find movies that contain parable-based lessons that you want to illustrate. Even if you choose a movie your students haven't seen, you can still use it. Just tell the story and let your students discover the lesson wrapped within it.

• Television—What's the most popular show on television right now? Why is it so popular? In the answer to that question,

"Jesus knew us enough to know that he should use examples that were familiar to people. And I think that's such an interesting thing because as a teacher, he knew he had to take people where they were. They understood pearls and nets and things like that. Then he took those things and said, 'Make a leap.'"
—Joani Schultz

you'll likely find a lesson to teach. And the TV programs provide the parables you need to get that lesson across more effectively.

• News and the Media—Read your paper and watch a few news programs each week. They're rich in parables, and the lessons contained in them are even better than movies or television because they're based on real life.

• Personal Experiences—Your own experiences can provide a wealth of materials from which you can construct terrific parables. You can also use real-life stories from your students or other people you know (with their permission, of course!).

• The Bible—Besides the parables Jesus used, you can find parables elsewhere in the Bible, even in the Old Testament. Who can forget the story Nathan told David that exposed David's sin with Bathsheba? Or what about the parable of the vineyard Isaiah used to condemn Israel's sin against God? Old parables like these can still teach us many lessons about what it means to follow God.

• Music—Popular songs often contain stories that illustrate a lesson. In fact, many of the songs we hear today are basically parables put to music. What a powerful tool for teaching!

> *"God has so designed creation that if you look, you can find the gospel locked up in the seasons of what he's done; even, in some ways, in the brutality of what we see in nature. That's not by accident either."*
>
> —Rick Lawrence

• Nature—God has provided many parables in nature. For example, the way a caterpillar turns into a butterfly. Or the way an eagle teaches its young to fly. Or the way a tree's roots go deeper in winter than in summer. All of these "acts of nature" are also parables about life. Use them!

Once you've collected the "raw material" for your parables, you're just a few steps away from creating a modern-day parable that you can use again and again. Let's go through an example together to see how easy it is to use parables in your teaching.

Based on the "raw material" you've collected, let's say you've come across a story you think conveys some interesting lessons about life. The story is about a boy whose arm is cut in a fight with a classmate. The wound is deep, but because the boy doesn't want to admit the other boy hurt him, he pretends the cut isn't that serious and does nothing to treat it. Within days, the cut gets infected, and the boy is forced to go to the emergency room for help.

That's your basic story. To create your finished parable, just follow these steps:

1. Find the life lesson or principle in the parable that you want to highlight. Many parables have multiple lessons hidden within them. That's OK. Just choose one lesson that you want to emphasize.

Let's practice with an example. Based on the story, let's say you want students to understand this principle: "When you refuse to forgive others, you end up only hurting yourself."

2. State the lesson as a maxim. Use the resources we've suggested for finding a maxim that fits your parable, or create one of your own using the definitions highlighted at the beginning of the chapter (p. 70-71). For our example, let's try personification: "Unforgiveness makes the heart sick."

3. Tie your parable to a specific Scripture passage. Not only does this act as a "check" to insure your parable is biblically accurate, it also can help you later when trying to think of a way to illustrate a particular Bible verse or passage. For our example, we might use Matthew 6:14 or Matthew 18:23-35.

4. Test your parable on a friend. Tell the story a few times to work out the kinks, and ask for feedback. Then fine-tune the story line to make it as effective as possible.

For our example, after some fine-tuning, this was the result:

There was a boy who once spread awful lies about his brother, simply because he didn't like him. When the brother heard of it, he got very angry and went to beat up the boy to make him stop his lies.

When he found his brother, he said, "You've been spreading lies about me for no good reason. It's time somebody taught you a lesson!" Then he swung his fist to strike the boy in the face.

But even though the boy was smaller than his brother, he was quick and crafty. He dodged his brother's fist, then pulled out a knife he had hidden beneath his shirt and cut his brother on the arm. Then he quickly ran away.

The cut was deep, but the brother was so angry at losing the fight that he didn't feel any pain. For the next several days, he did nothing at all to tend the injury. All he could think about was how he was going to get back at his brother who had cut him. But after several days had passed, the brother's arm became infected. He got a terrible fever and had to be taken to the hospital. When he finally saw the seriousness of his injury, he forgot all about his anger against his brother. "If I had focused on tending to my arm instead of holding a grudge, I would never have ended up here. As it is, I have become terribly ill."

In the same way, unforgiveness makes your heart sick. But if you forgive those who injure you—even when they injure without cause—your heart will stay healthy and strong.

5. Write it down! This is so important, not only because it helps you perfect the story even more, but it's also an essential step for creating a parable notebook. You can arrange your parables by topic or by Scripture reference, but do keep them on file! You can use them again and again to help your students understand important life lessons. Although any sort of notebook will work, we've provided a "Parable Dream Sheet" on page 90 that you can photocopy and use as a tool for recording your parables.

Finally, as you begin using parables and maxims in your teaching, consider the following tips:

• Don't always explain your parables. Although Jesus often explained his parables (especially to his disciples), sometimes he didn't. Instead, he let the parable speak for itself and allowed room for his listeners to process the parable's meaning on their own. Doing this in a modern classroom may seem awkward at first, but it can be very effective at encouraging students to think for themselves.

• Vary your delivery methods. Don't always present a parable in the same way. Besides simply telling the story, try using video or audio clips, or on-the-spot dramas to tell the parable for you.

• Let your students practice telling parables too. Many of your students may have "teaching stories" from which the whole class can gain important life lessons. Make time for others to share their own "parables" with the group.

As a teacher, Jesus is probably known more for his use of parables and sayings than any other teaching method he employed. As Christian teachers who want to follow in his steps, we can be known as "parable teachers" too. All it takes is a little imagination, an awareness of what's happening in the world around us, and a solid understanding of the truths God would want us to teach. And the payoff is far more than just an interesting story—it can be changed lives.

[1] H. Jackson Brown Jr., *Life's Little Instruction Book, Volume III* (Nashville, TN: Rutledge Hill Press, Inc., 1995), #1536.

[2] Brown, *Life's Little Instruction Book, Volume II* (Nashville, TN: Rutledge Hill Press, Inc., 1993), #870.

[3] Brown, *Life's Little Instruction Book, Volume III*, #1313.

[4] Brown, *Life's Little Instruction Book, Volume II*, #603.

[5] Vine's Expository Dictionary of Biblical Words, ed. by W.E. Vine, Merrill F. Unger, and William White, Jr. (Nashville, TN: Thomas Nelson Publishers, 1985), 18-19.

[6] William Barclay, *The Mind of Jesus* (New York, NY: Harper & Row, 1961), 92.

[7] Ibid., 95.

[8] Compiled from reference materials in the Disciple's Study Bible (Nashville: Holman Bible Publishers, 1988) and the Ryrie Study Bible (Chicago: Moody Bible Institute, 1978).

[9] Story adapted from "Show Them What You Mean" in *Illustrations Unlimited*, ed. by James S. Hewett, (Wheaton, IL: Tyndale House Publishers, 1988), 107. Used by permission. All rights reserved.

[10] Barclay, *The Mind of Jesus*, 93.

[11] Roy B. Zuck, *Teaching as Jesus Taught* (Grand Rapids, MI: Baker Books, 1995), 312.

Parable Dream Sheet

Parable Topic: _____

1. What's the "raw material" for this parable? (It could be from movies, television, news and the media, the Bible, personal experience, nature, or something else.)

2. What's the life lesson or principle you want to highlight? (State it as a maxim if possible.)

3. What Bible passage can you tie to this lesson?

4. Write your finished parable below:

Chapter 5
Discourses, Discussions, and Debates

"Now when he saw the crowds, he
went up on a mountainside and sat down.
His disciples came to him,
and he began to teach them, saying..."
—Matthew 5:1-2

What would happen if you walked into your youth or adult class, sat down, and said this?

Your religious leaders hold positions of authority under God, so you should follow their advice and do what they say. But don't do what they do, for they do not practice what they preach. Today's religious leaders put horrible burdens on people's shoulders—burdens God never intended people to have. But these leaders of yours are not willing to even lift a finger to help you bear up under the weight.

Everything they do, they do to feed their own egos and to get noticed by other people. In fact, they love to be recognized in public and to rub elbows with famous people who are part of the "in" crowd.

But you should not be like them. If you want to be "great," then become a servant to all those around you. For whoever exalts himself will be humbled, and whoever humbles himself will be exalted.

Payback time is coming, you religious leaders, you hypocrites! For you conceal the true way to God's kingdom. Not only do you fail to enter, but you also prevent others from entering as well.

Payback time is coming, you religious leaders, you hypocrites! You'll go thousands of miles to make a convert, but then you turn around and make him twice as much the son of hell that you are...

Payback time is coming, you religious leaders, you hypocrites! You are like a spotless casket, which looks beautiful on the outside, but inside is full of death and the stench of decay. In the same way, you appear to people as righteous but on the inside you are full of hypocrisy and evil...

You snakes! You family of vipers! How will you escape being condemned to hell?

Not your typical Sunday school lecture, is it? But this *is* an example of "lecture"—Jesus' style. This paraphrase is based on Jesus' discourse of the "seven woes" against the Pharisees found in Matthew 23:1-39, but Jesus presented many other similar lectures or discourses, and all of them made a significant impact on his listeners. Although biblical scholars disagree about the number of discourses Jesus gave, all would agree that it was a key aspect of his role as a teacher.

For a listing of Jesus' discourses, see the "Jesus' Discourses" box below. That listing includes only those lectures in which Jesus was speaking to more than one person, and it excludes any sections in which he used parables. Regardless of how you count them, Jesus' lectures make up a key part of the Gospel record. And, as we'll see, Jesus used lecture both for practical and educational reasons.

Teacher's Corner: Don't Forget Parables

Parables were certainly a key element in Jesus' lectures. But since we already discussed Jesus' use of parables in Chapter 4, we'll limit our discussion in this chapter to the other techniques Jesus used in his lectures and debates.

Jesus' Discourses

Lecture Topic	Reference
Sermon on the Mount	Matthew 5:2–7:27; Luke 6:20-49
Commissioning the Twelve	Matthew 10:5-42; Luke 9:3-5
John the Baptist	Matthew 11:7-19; Luke 7:24-35
Judgment on cities	Matthew 11:20-24
Blasphemy	Matthew 12:25-45; Mark 3:23-29; Luke 11:17-36
Discipleship	Matthew 16:24-28
Greatest in the Kingdom	Matthew 18:3-11
Forgiveness	Matthew 18:15-20
Pharisees	Matthew 23:1-39; Mark 12:38-40; Luke 20:45-47
Jesus' second coming	Matthew 24:4-44
Saving and losing life	Mark 8:34-38; Luke 9:23-27

Commissioning the seventy-two	Luke 10:2-24
Prayer	Luke 11:2-13
Pharisees	Luke 11:37-52
Hypocrisy	Luke 12:1-12
Worry	Luke 12:22-34
Family divisions	Luke 12:49-53
Discernment of the times	Luke 12:54-59
Exclusion from the Kingdom	Luke 13:22-30
Offenses	Luke 17:1-6
The coming Kingdom	Luke 17:20-37
True greatness	Luke 22:24-30
Sowing and reaping	John 4:31-38
Jesus as the source of life	John 5:19-47
Gate and Shepherd	John 10:1-18
Jesus' death	John 12:23-36
Abiding in Christ	John 15:1–16:16

Along with lecture, another tool Jesus used in his teaching was discussion or debate. In fact, discussions and debates sometimes went hand in hand with Jesus' lectures or parables. Jesus occasionally paired together lectures and parables with discussion or debate to add variety to his teaching and increase his effectiveness. Here's a listing of Jesus' discussions and debates recorded in the Gospels. Those marked with an asterisk (*) either precede or follow one of Jesus' lectures or parables. Look up and read through a few of these to see how Jesus used lectures, discussions, and debates together to maximize their effectiveness.

Jesus' Discussions and Debates

Topic	Reference
Traditions of the elders	Matthew 15:1-20; Mark 7:1-23
Jesus' identity	Matthew 16:13-20; Luke 9:18-27
Temple tax	Matthew 17:24-27
Marriage and divorce	Matthew 19:3-12; Mark 10:2-12
Riches in heaven and earth	Matthew 19:16-30; Mark 10:17-31; Luke 18:18-30
False ambition and servanthood	Matthew 20:23-28; Mark 10:39-45

Faith and prayer	Matthew 21:21-22; Mark 11:20-26
Jesus' authority*	Matthew 21:23-27; Mark 11:27-33; Luke 20:1-8
Taxes*	Matthew 22:15-22; Mark 12:13-17; Luke 20:20-26
Resurrection*	Matthew 22:23-33; Mark 12:18-27; Luke 20:27-38
The greatest commandment*	Matthew 22:34-40; Mark 12:28-34
The Christ*	Matthew 22:41-46; Mark 12:35-37; Luke 20:41-44
Fasting	Mark 2:18-22; Luke 5:33-35
The Sabbath	Mark 2:23-28; Luke 6:1-5
Jesus and Beelzebub	Mark 3:20-35
Being born again	John 3:1-21
The bread of life	John 6:25-59
The source of Jesus' message	John 7:14-24
Validity of Jesus' testimony	John 8:12-30
Spiritual freedom	John 8:31-58
Jesus' oneness with the Father*	John 10:22-38
Jesus' departure*	John 13:31–14:31
The disciples' grief*	John 16:19-33

The Problem With Lecture in Modern Teaching

In our society, "lecture" has become synonymous with boredom. The term conjures up images of talking heads frozen behind elevated podiums, and listeners seated with folded arms, their own heads bobbing up and down as they fight to stay awake. The media promotes this caricature as well. Who among us doesn't know the voice of Charlie Brown's schoolteacher? That nameless, faceless, off-screen voice we hear that only drones, "blah, blah...blah, blah...blah, blah-blah." The same image of a nonsensical, out-of-touch educator is often promoted in our movies and in television. Education by lecture has almost become a contradiction in terms. "Death by lecture" might be a better reflection of our society's feelings on the subject.

This criticism of modern-day lecture is largely deserved. Of all the teaching methods available to us, lecture can be the most abused. And, unfortunately, it often is. For one thing, lecture is the easiest way to convey a lot of information in a short amount of time. If your goal as a teacher is to "dump information" onto your students, straight lecture can seem like the best way to go. After all, you can convey a lot more material in a shorter amount of time if you don't have to worry about being interrupted or sharing control of the classroom with your students.

> *"If you're lecturing to a group of people, you have very little feedback—you have very little evidence as to what's going on with all the people, and the problem is that the teacher can get away with the thought that 'I'm connecting with 100 percent of the students.'"*
> —Thom Schultz

Unfortunately, there are two problems with this idea.

First, and most importantly, it is a mistake to believe that our goal as teachers is ever to simply "dump information" on people. Nothing could be further from the truth! Our goal goes far beyond conveying information. We want to provoke learning and impact lives. To what end? Remember Principle 2.

Principle 2

The ultimate goal of Christian teaching is to draw people into a genuine, personal relationship with God.

Seeing lecture simply as a tool for conveying information misses the point of our teaching altogether. In fact, Jesus never used lecture simply as an "information dump." He often used it for a different reason completely. (More on that in a moment.)

The second problem with using lecture simply as a way to convey information is that it's ineffective. As Thom and Joani Schultz write:

> The medium—straight speaking to a crowd—results in very little retention, very little learning. According to the publication *Communication Briefings*, people forget 40 percent of a speaker's message within 20 minutes. They forget 60 percent after a half day. And after a week they lose 90 percent. These figures apply to gifted speakers as well as lackluster ones. No matter how articulate the speaker, almost everything he or she utters is quickly forgotten, forever lost and never applied by the vast majority of listeners.[1]

If lecture is so ineffective, why use it at all? And, more importantly, why did Jesus—the Master Teacher—use it *so often?*

Some might say that even though lecture is ineffective, Jesus used it for cultural reasons. In Jesus' time, and in many Middle Eastern cultures today, "a 'pecking order' of seniority exists in virtually every social setting, and the expectation is that juniors will listen in silent submission if a senior speaks, as indeed the disciples do with their Master. To do otherwise would be considered shameful."[2] Therefore, some educators believe that Jesus lectured simply because it was culturally appropriate—even though he no doubt knew that lecture was ineffective as a teaching tool. But does that sound like something that Jesus—the Master Teacher—would do?

As we pointed out in Chapter 1, Jesus never let culture control his choice of teaching methods. If a method worked, he used it, whether it was culturally appropriate or not. Therefore, even though lecture was the way people expected Jesus to teach, he would not have used it unless it was effective.

So now we're faced with a quandary: Is lecture effective, or isn't it? Maybe this story can help us find an answer:

There was a man who grew up in a simple tribe deep in the jungle. In all his years, he had never seen modern cities or technology. But one day an explorer from Switzerland came into the man's village. The man saw an incredible jewel on his wrist, and he asked the explorer what it was.

"A genuine Swiss watch," responded the explorer.

The explorer eventually left, but the man couldn't forget the beautiful jewel the explorer possessed and soon decided he must get one for himself. So he left his village and traveled to Switzerland, where he found a watch shop, and used the last of his gold to buy a genuine Swiss watch.

"Do you want the instruction book?" asked the salesman.

"No," said the man. "It looks simple enough to wear."

And so the man put the watch on his wrist and admired it as he walked around town. Soon, however, his wrist became uncomfortable, and he thought, "Wouldn't the jewel look better on my ankle?" So he tried to put the watch around his ankle, but the watchband was too small. So the man removed the watchband, found a string, and tied the watch around his ankle so that it dangled on the ground as he walked. He thought the tinkling noise would make people notice his jewel all the more. But the more he walked, the more he damaged the watch. Eventually it stopped working and lost its luster, and the man threw it in a ditch.

Lecture can be an effective and powerful teaching tool, unless it's used for the wrong reasons in the wrong way. Then it becomes useless, good for nothing but to be cast into the trash.

So we've answered the first question—lecture *is* an effective teaching tool, as long as it's used in the right way and for the right reasons. But what are the right *reasons* for using lecture? And what is the right *way* to go about it?

Perhaps we can discover the answer to those questions by examining a third question: Why do people remember movies better than they remember sermons?

Think about it. When did you last hear a sermon? A week ago? A few days? How much of it can you remember? If you're lucky, you might remember the main points (if you took notes). But if you're like most people, you don't remember much at all.

Now think about the last time you saw a movie. How long ago was that? a week? a month? How much of that movie can you recall? Do you remember the story line? Probably. Do any scenes stick out in your mind? Most likely. Do you recall any moral or lesson the movie conveyed? Absolutely (assuming it had one, of course)!

So what's the difference? In both situations you were seated passively in a crowd, observing what was going on in the front of the room. You were not conversing directly with the teacher or the movie screen. And yet you remember far more of the movie than you do of the sermon. Why?

In response, people might say things like this:

"Movies are more visually stimulating. They give you a variety of things to look at and take in."

"Movies tell stories, and stories are easier to remember."

"Movies are designed to entertain more than teach, so the moviemakers often spend a lot more time and money focusing on dazzling, memorable effects than on the movie's content."

In those responses and others like them, you'll find not only the difference between movies and most lectures, but also several hints to understanding what lecture is really for, and what it takes to make lecture an effective tool in your teaching—just like Jesus.

How Jesus Used Lectures, Discussions, and Debates

"The medium is the message." It's a common saying among communicators and marketers these days—a truism that essentially means that the way you deliver your message is as important as the message itself. The truth is, when it comes to most forms of communication, including lecture, the medium can be *more* important than the message.

> Communication scholars understand the medium. A University of California study found that the words speakers so carefully choose actually carry a minimal part of the message. How the speaker sounds (inflection, tonality, voice variety, emphasis, and energy) communicates 38 percent of the message. And what the listeners see carries 55 percent of the message. This includes the speaker's appearance, gestures, movement and visual aids. Only 7 percent of the message that listeners receive comes from the words themselves.[3]

So these movie-makers who spend so much time and energy on the *delivery* of their "message" may understand a secret of learning that most modern lecturers don't: The medium *matters!*

Some speakers describe this relationship between "medium" and "message" as a rocket carrying a payload. The payload is the message. The rocket, with it's fuel and booster system, is the medium. No matter how good or needed the payload might be, it will never arrive at its destination without a sufficiently powerful rocket to carry it.

Of course, Jesus understood the vital connection between message and medium. Although we don't have the benefit of video clips or sound bites to actually see and hear what Jesus did in his lectures and debates, we can read about the effect his lectures and discussions had on his listeners. And from those reactions, we can draw some solid conclusions about why and how Jesus used lectures and debates to draw people into relationships with God.

Conclusion #1: *Jesus used lecture and debate to reveal truths about himself—not just about his topic.*

When Jesus finished his famous Sermon on the Mount, the Bible says "the crowds were amazed at his teaching" (Matthew 7:28b). But why were they amazed? Was it because...

- his teaching was new and innovative?
- he made claims about himself and God that no other teacher did?
- his teaching gave a deeper understanding of what it means to follow God?

Although all of these things are true about Jesus' teaching, the Bible records none of them as reasons why people were amazed at his teaching. What does Scripture say amazed them? Jesus himself.

"When Jesus had finished saying these things, the crowds were amazed at his teaching, because he taught *as one who had authority,* and not as their teachers of the law" (Matthew 7:28-29, author emphasis).

And again,

"Then he went down to Capernaum, a town in Galilee, and on the Sabbath began to teach the people. They were amazed at his teaching, *because his message had authority*" (Luke 4:31-32, author emphasis).

Jesus' lectures or discourses focused on powerful truths about God and humanity. Yet when it was all said and done, the one "revelation" people came away with most was about Jesus himself. It's as if they walked away from his lectures, saying, "Wow! This teacher really speaks with authority! There's something different about him. He's not like the other teachers I've heard."

When you think about it, doesn't that sound typical? Think again back to the last sermon you heard. But rather than try to remember what the topic was, see if you can recall your impressions of the speaker. The pastor at my church is so animated in his presentation each Sunday that some people have cautioned him not to stand so close to the steps, because they fear he will fall off. I can't tell you what he talked about last week, but I can tell you he's terribly passionate and bold about what he believes. The same experiences were true of Jesus' listeners. They naturally remembered more about the man than they did his message. In fact, in most if not all of Jesus' lectures, Jesus probably *was* the ultimate message he was trying to convey—regardless of the topic.

Let me explain what I mean. People may have remembered every word of Jesus' teaching, and rightly so, because his teaching was true and holy. But what probably caused most people to follow Jesus wasn't simply that they agreed with the lessons he taught. Rather, it was their awe and admiration for Jesus himself that compelled them to follow him. Lectures have a way of revealing more than just your topic to an audience. They can also reveal your heart. Jesus understood this principle and purposefully used lecture to reveal *his heart* to people.

When it comes to discussions and debates, Jesus' purpose becomes even more clear, because many of his debates and discussions actually revolved around some aspect of his own identity or personal character.

For example, consider this debate Jesus had with the Pharisees, recorded in John 8:12-19, 21-30. As you read it, think about how Jesus purposefully used this debate as a means to reveal his character and identity to those who listened.

> When Jesus spoke again to the people, he said, "I am the light of the world. Whoever follows me will never walk in darkness, but will have the light of life."
>
> The Pharisees challenged him, "Here you are, appearing as your own witness; your testimony is not valid."
>
> Jesus answered, "Even if I testify on my own behalf, my testimony is valid, for I know where I came from and where I am going. But you have no idea where I come from or where I am going. You judge by human standards; I pass judgment on no one. But if I do judge, my decisions are right, because I am not alone. I stand with the Father, who sent me. In your own Law it is written that the testimony of two men is valid. I am one who testifies for myself; my other witness is the Father, who sent me."
>
> Then they asked him, "Where is your father?"
>
> "You do not know me or my Father," Jesus replied. "If you knew me, you would know my Father also."
>
> Once more Jesus said to them, "I am going away, and you will look for me, and you will die in your sin. Where I go, you cannot come."
>
> This made the Jews ask, "Will he kill himself? Is that why he says, 'Where I go, you cannot come'?"
>
> But he continued, "You are from below; I am from above. You are of this world; I am not of this world. I told you that you would die in your sins; if you do not believe that I am the one I claim to be, you will indeed die in your sins."

"Who are you?" they asked.

"Just what I have been claiming all along," Jesus replied. "I have much to say in judgment of you. But he who sent me is reliable, and what I have heard from him I tell the world."

They did not understand that he was telling them about his Father. So Jesus said, "When you have lifted up the Son of Man, then you will know that I am the one I claim to be, and that I do nothing on my own but speak just what the Father has taught me. The one who sent me is with me; he has not left me alone, for I always do what pleases him." Even as he spoke, many put their faith in him.

Teacher's Corner: A Word About "Discussion"

When modern teachers talk about discussion, we are normally referring to a type of discussion sometimes called a "round-table" discussion, in which a moderator facilitates the equal contributions of several people's opinions on a particular subject.

Although this is an effective and powerful teaching tool, it is not the same kind of discussion that we're talking about in this chapter. (That kind of round-table discussion will be addressed in Chapter 7.) In this chapter, we're highlighting those discussions or debates in which the teacher's opinion or teaching is the primary focus of conversation. This type of discussion can perhaps be most easily compared to a "Question and Answer" session that modern speakers sometimes use to either follow or precede their lectures. Instead of a round-table approach, this kind of discussion is more of a "one against several" scenario in which one person (Jesus) is clarifying or debating the validity of his teaching in front of a group of several listeners (the disciples or the Pharisees).

As we examine Jesus' "discussions" in this chapter, be sure to keep this distinction in mind.

In any lecture or debate, people will remember some of what you teach or say. And a few will take what you've said and effectively apply it to their lives. But for most people, the one thing they'll remember long after the details of your lecture are forgotten is...*you.* They'll remember your passion, your demeanor and attitude—even the way you carry yourself in front of a group. That's the impression people will carry with them. And that's where some of the most effective teaching in lecture can happen.

In Jesus' case, this notion that "the medium is the message" was ultimately true. Jesus was the Word of God made flesh (John 1:14). He didn't just come to show the way; he was the Way (John 14:6). When Jesus lectured or debated, his goal went beyond revealing the truth about whatever topic he was talking about. His goal was to reveal the truth about *himself*. He (the medium) *was* the message (salvation).

But what about us today? As Christian teachers, how should we use lecture, discussion, and debate in our classrooms? Some might say that, like Jesus, our goal should be to reveal our own hearts through our discourses. After all, wouldn't our students benefit from seeing our passion for a cause or our anger over the injustices we see in the world around us?

Although this is a noble goal, I do not believe it is the best goal for us as modern lecturers and discussion leaders. Our goal is not to draw attention to ourselves, but rather to focus our students' attention on Christ. He is the one we want students to relate to. So instead of using lecture, discussion, and debate only to reveal insights about us, we should use it to reveal insights about the life of Christ *in* us.

Principle 5
Use lecture to reveal Jesus—*not just your topic.*

As Paul wrote in Galatians 2:20, "I have been crucified with Christ and I no longer live, but Christ lives in me. The life I live in the body, I live by faith in the Son of God, who loved me and gave himself for me."

We, too, "no longer live," but Jesus lives in us. As teachers, we can use lecture and discussion for more than simply conveying information. We can use it to reveal Jesus through us.

How can we do this? Really, it's easier than you might think. With a humble heart and a willingness to be vulnerable, any Christian can use lecture and debate in the same way Jesus did—to reveal *Christ*. To help you get started, follow these simple guidelines for using lecture and discussion in your own classroom.

1. Never use lecture simply as a way to "dump information." I know we've already made this point, but it's so important that it bears repeating. If you have information to convey, and you want that information to be the sole focus of your students' attention, don't use straight lecture to do it. If you do, your students may be watching *you*, but not necessarily

focusing on what you're saying. Instead, convey the information by guiding students through a real-life experience or by sharing a parable.

"Who you are is way more of a lesson than what you teach, or what you say, or what's in your lesson plan."

—Joani Schultz

2. Regardless of your topic, present your lecture or discussion in a way that reveals Jesus. As I've stated, how you present or debate your teaching typically makes a more memorable impact on people than the teaching itself. So in your lectures and discussions, be aware that you represent Christ in everything you say and do. Ask God to help you be passionate about the things Jesus is passionate about, joyful over the things that bring him joy, and sad about the things that make him sad. Pray for God's Spirit to show students the truth about Christ through your personality and presentation.

Sometimes, of course, you won't feel capable of letting Jesus shine through you. We all have days when we feel weak or when our hearts are troubled. When that happens, don't be afraid to be vulnerable with your students. Reveal your own anger or confusion about a topic or event. Ask students to pray for you—to help you focus your attention on God. And ask God to reveal himself through you even in your weakness. By being vulnerable, you can let God use your character and personality to impact others positively toward Christ.

Conclusion #2: *Jesus used lecture and debate to demonstrate that he knew his audience.*

No one who has studied Jesus' debates and lectures to any degree could ever claim that he was timid or feared what people would think of him. To the contrary, Jesus seemed to welcome controversy and never shied away from confrontations or debates that involved defending himself or exposing the wrongful actions or beliefs of his audience. Such was the case when the Pharisees tried to discredit Jesus because he didn't hold to their empty traditions. Let's drop in on the debate that's recorded in Mark 7:5-15. As you read, compare Jesus' debate style with your own as a teacher. What are your similarities? What are your differences?

So the Pharisees and teachers of the law asked Jesus, "Why don't your disciples live according to the tradition of the elders instead of eating their food with 'unclean' hands?"

He replied, "Isaiah was right when he prophesied about you hypocrites; as it is written:

" 'These people honor me with their lips, but their hearts are far from me. They worship me in vain; their teachings are but rules taught by men.'

"You have let go of the commands of God and are holding on to the traditions of men."

And he said to them: "You have a fine way of setting aside the commands of God in order to observe your own traditions! For Moses said, 'Honor your father and your mother,' and, 'Anyone who curses his father or mother must be put to death.' But you say that if a man says to his father or mother: 'Whatever help you might otherwise have received from me is Corban' (that is, a gift devoted to God), then you no longer let him do anything for his father or mother. Thus you nullify the word of God by your tradition that you have handed down. And you do many things like that."

Again Jesus called the crowd to him and said, "Listen to me, everyone, and understand this. Nothing outside a man can make him 'unclean' by going into him. Rather, it is what comes out of a man that makes him 'unclean.' "

Of course, the Pharisees were antagonists bent on discrediting Jesus' teaching and authority. And although most of us as teachers have encountered rebellious children or cynical adults in our classes, we probably haven't had to deal directly with such harsh opposition. Nevertheless, Jesus' example demonstrates how he used debates and lectures as a way to expose his complete understanding of his audience. It's as though he is saying, "I know who you are. I know what you're doing. And you can't hide yourself from me." Sometimes that understanding brings comfort (as in Jesus' discussion with his disciples in John 14), and sometimes it brings conviction (as in this encounter between Jesus and the Pharisees).

Why is it important to convey to your students that you understand them? There are two very important reasons:

• Understanding your students is the first essential step toward teaching them anything. Marketers and public relations experts know that they must understand their audience before they can effectively attempt to persuade them to do anything. In a similar way, we as teachers must understand our students—what they feel, what they struggle with, how they think, and what they want—before we can hope to teach them anything about God. Jesus was expert at perceiving the needs and wants of the people around him, and using those desires as a launching point toward a discourse or discussion about God's truth. As those who want to follow in his steps, we must do the same.

How? As a starting point, in Chapter 9 you'll find a helpful questionnaire you can use with your students (p. 184). You can use the information you gather as an important first step toward understanding your students better. In addition, you can read through a few of the discourses and debates compiled in this chapter. Focus on how Jesus used people's needs and desires as a launching point for learning. Then try a similar approach in your own classroom, focusing on the needs and desires you have discovered.

• If your students don't think you understand them or where they're at, they won't listen to you. Have you ever tried to share your faith with a drug addict who's living on the streets? The first time I ever attempted it, I failed miserably, because the drug addict I was talking to didn't believe I could understand him or relate to where he was at. He dismissed my experience with God's salvation as a nice, comfortable delusion that people with nice, comfortable lives bring on themselves. After all, I have never been addicted to drugs, and I've never been homeless. How could I know what life was really like for him? And how could I have the arrogance to claim that Jesus was the answer he sought?

Of course, it wasn't necessary for me to become a drug addict or live on the streets in order to understand that man's needs or desires. Whether we're addicts or homeless or rich or "comfortable," all of us share the same fundamental needs and desires as human beings. I may not know what it's like to live on the streets, but I do know (as many of us do) what it's like to feel "homeless." But even though I may have understood the addict's needs and desires, he still rejected my message because I failed to *convince him* that I understood.

That's why Jesus used teaching tools like lecture and debate to demonstrate his understanding of the people he addressed. He knew the importance of convincing people that he understood them, so they would have no excuse for ignoring his teaching. As Christian teachers, we, too, must convince our students that we understand them if we hope to reach them with our teaching. How? Although there are many ways, here's one technique a pastor used to stay in touch with his congregation. As you'll see, it would be easy to adapt his technique to a classroom situation.

> One pastor utilizes a "sermon squad." This group of six or eight laypeople receives Scripture passages the pastor will be preaching on for the ensuing six months. Every Wednesday they complete and submit a brief questionnaire about the following Sunday's Scripture. The questions are quite simple: "What questions does this Scripture raise in your mind? What's happened to you lately that this Scripture speaks to? What changes need to take place in you and our members as a result of reading this Scripture?" These folks take their weekly responsibility seriously because they know the pastor uses their insights in his preaching. Every six months, a new set of members makes up the "sermon squad."[4]

Of course, understanding our students can sometimes act as a two-edged sword. Occasionally our understanding will lead us to confront our students by teaching them things they *need* to learn, even when they don't want to. That's why, in addition to listening to our students' needs and desires, we also need to stay focused on God's Word and faithfully teach the truths it contains—even when those truths may be hard for our students to hear.

Teacher's Corner:
What About Using Lecture With Children?

Many modern educators would be quick to say that lecture is an inappropriate tool to use with younger kids, for a whole host of reasons:

- Kids can't focus on the speaker's words for very long.
- Kids can't sit still for very long.
- Kids can't understand the abstract concepts that often come up in a lecture format.
- Kids need to be able to interact with the teacher and each other in order to learn.

But what if you could create a short lecture (say, seven minutes or less) that avoided all of the pitfalls listed above? Then could you use lecture in teaching younger kids? You bet!

Here are some tips on creating an effective children's "lecture," gleaned from Thom and Joani Schultz's book *Why Nobody Learns Much of Anything at Church: And How to Fix It.* Try using these pointers to help you create an effective lecture to use with children:

● Assume nothing. Since children think in concrete terms, never use churchy jargon, or abstract words that kids can easily misunderstand. And when you do try to explain hard-to-grasp concepts—like the Trinity—carefully illustrate them in concrete ways so kids can understand on their own level. For example, when explaining the Trinity, you might show kids an egg (which has three parts, but is one egg); or show them water, ice, and steam (which are three forms of the same substance).

● Make one point. "Less is more" when speaking to children. Instead of trying to make several points in your lecture, make only one point, repeating it over and over in simple language. For greater effectiveness, make the point into a maxim to help kids remember it more easily.

● Appeal to the senses. Children learn best when we involve more than one of their senses. So when you're speaking to younger kids, use props they can look at, sounds they can hear, fuzzy objects to touch, sweets or salts to taste, and fragrances to smell. Engaging multiple senses will involve the kids in your teaching and greatly enhance learning.

● Allow time for give and take. Include a time for questions and discussion at some point in your talk, just as Jesus often did. Ask the children questions about what you talked about, and invite questions from them. This interactive format helps keep their minds focused and makes learning blossom.[5]

Conclusion #3: *Jesus' lectures and debates got his listeners involved.*

Thom Schultz, CEO of Group Publishing, Inc., has said, "As a teacher, Jesus was always looking for an occasion to get people's attention in an astonishing way in order to provide a platform to teach. His approach reminds me of one of the adult teachers at our church, who put us to work on a project, then sneaked to the back of the room and took the door and just slammed it! Whoa! Boy, it got us. It woke us up and got our brains in gear, and then he drew a lesson out of that…That's what Jesus did. He injected into a brain-dead environment a surprise to get people's attention and then learn from it."

We actually saw an example of this technique in the Mark 7:9-15 passage we read earlier. Did you notice it? Look again.

"And he said to them: 'You have a fine way of setting aside the commands of God in order to observe your own traditions! For Moses said, "Honor your father and your mother," and, "Anyone who curses his father or mother must be put to death." But you say that if a man says to his father or mother: "Whatever help you might otherwise have received from me is Corban" (that is, a gift devoted to God), then you no longer let him do anything for his father or mother. Thus you nullify the word of God by your tradition that you have handed down. And you do many things like that.' Again Jesus called the crowd to him and said, 'Listen to me, everyone, and understand this. Nothing outside a man can make him "unclean" by going into him. Rather, it is what comes out of a man that makes him "unclean." ' "

In this scene, Jesus is caught up in a debate with the Pharisees over what's "clean" and "unclean" for Jews. The argument attracts the attention of the crowds, and as the debate heats up, they listen in more intensely. Then Jesus, recognizing the teachable moment, shifts his focus from the Pharisees to the crowd and draws them into the debate. Suddenly, those who were passive observers are swept into the dialogue and become directly involved, providing them the opportunity to experience direct, genuine learning.

Another more forceful example of how Jesus involved listeners is recorded in John 13:1-17. In that passage, Jesus washes his disciples' feet, then goes on to teach them about loving and serving each other after he is gone. In educational circles, this kind of involving device is called a "direct personal experience" or simply "experiential learning." Jesus was a master at using real-life experiences as teaching tools in conjunction with parables, sayings, lectures, and debates—in order to draw people into learning and help them practically apply what they learn to their lives. It's an excellent tool for involving your students in your lectures or discussions, too.

For an example of an experiential learning activity that you can use in conjunction with lecture or debate, see the activity titled "Multiplied Talents" on page 109. This activity is taken from Mike and Amy Nappa's book *Bore No More!*, which is a collection of seventy different experiential activities designed to be used in combination with lecture or discussion.

In Chapter 6, we'll examine more closely Jesus' use of this technique to inspire learning in his listeners, and explore many other ways we can incorporate experiential learning in our teaching today.

Multiplied Talents

Topic: Using God's Gifts

Scripture: Luke 19:11-27

In April 1991, Charisma magazine reported an unusual happening. Instead of asking his congregation for money, Pastor Phil Derstine had given $5 each to 250 members of his church. These people had thirty days to follow the example of Luke 19:11-27 and multiply this gift. At the end of the month, the $1,250 investment came back as $10,000! Derstine's illustration was certainly risky, but it was an excellent way to bring the Scripture to life. You can follow Pastor Derstine's example and bring Luke 19:11-27 to life for your congregation.

You may need approval from the church treasurer to use funds for this idea. Or you may wish to use your own money and donate anything returned beyond your original investment to a specified charity. In either case, have the determined dollar amount ready to distribute at the end of your sermon.

Near the end of your sermon about Luke 19:11-27, offer a challenge to your congregation. Explain that you'd like to give them the same opportunity the master gave in Jesus' story by giving away money for the congregation to use. Tell congregation members the following guidelines:

• Everyone who accepts the money must "invest" it in some way that potentially could result in earnings of more than the original investment.

• The money can be invested in any creative way that you believe will bring a return within the specified time limit.

• All earnings must be turned in at the time limit to be used for (charity of your choice).

• You can't merely return the same money at the end of the time period.

Don't force anyone to participate, but challenge those who do want to be involved. Explain that you and your family will be participating as well. Set a specified time limit for people to turn in the results of their investments.

Suggest creative ways people can invest their funds. Offer examples such as these:

- Use the money to buy gas for your mower, then mow lawns for pay.
- Use the money to purchase craft supplies. Then sell the things you make using the supplies. (Several people who want to use this idea may want to get together and have a craft fair. The same idea could be done with baked items, with several joining for a bake sale.)
- Use the money to get advertisements printed for a sports tournament. Charge a fee per person or team entering the event.

When everyone understands the guidelines, distribute the money. Then close your sermon with a commissioning prayer, asking God to bless the efforts of the people who took the challenge.

At the end of the specified time limit, have those who participated turn in their earnings during a worship service. Have several people tell about their investment experiences and the results.

(Note: Some people may end up with nothing to show for their investments. Let these people know that you appreciate their efforts anyway!)

Complete the project by reminding people that God has given us more than money to invest. We should be investing God's gifts wisely in many areas of life—in our families, our friends, our community, and so on. Ask everyone to consider this question as they leave: When the time comes, what return will I have to bring God on all the gifts he has given me?

Variation: In 1994, Dr. Norm Wakefield wanted to try this idea but didn't have the large cash amount needed for everyone in his congregation. He used $16 instead. Here's how you can do what he did:

Take three envelopes and put $10 in one, $5 in another, and $1 in the third. Randomly tape the envelopes under seats. Then issue the challenge and have people check under their seats to see if they've received the gifts. Have everyone who finds an envelope take the challenge.

Or use the $16 and simply distribute the money to the first three people who come forward to accept the challenge. Make all the guidelines the same.[6]

Conclusion #4: *Jesus used stories and visual aids to make his lectures and discussions memorable.*

Remember our question about what makes movies more memorable than most lectures? One obvious difference is that movies contain far more visual aids and have story lines that help people remember what they've seen and heard. Of course, movie-makers accomplish that feat by spending many millions of dollars on special effects and huge salaries to attract the best actors and writers. Unless you've recently won the lottery, you probably don't have access to those kinds of resources to make your lectures and discussions more memorable. But the great news is that you don't need lots of money to make your lectures and discussions "stick" in people's minds. After all, did Jesus have lots of money to spend on his presentation techniques? No. Were his lectures and discussions memorable? Well, we're still talking about them two thousand years later, so I'd say they were. How did Jesus do it? And how can we?

In Chapter 4, we discussed how Jesus used parables and stories to make his teaching memorable. Often his lectures were either preceded or followed by parables. He often used stories to introduce a topic, emphasize a point, or answer a question. These stories have a way of sticking in your mind, so that you continue to glean lessons from them long after the teaching session has ended.

Jesus also used visual aids frequently in his lectures. Just picture the scene in Matthew 18 where his disciples come to him and ask, "Who is the greatest in the kingdom of heaven?" Jesus didn't simply answer the question. Instead, he used a visual aid—a little boy—to drive the point home.

"He called a little child and had him stand among them. And he said, 'I tell you the truth, unless you change and become like little children, you will never enter the kingdom of heaven. Therefore, whoever humbles himself like this child is the greatest in the kingdom of heaven' " (Matthew 18:2-4).

What a powerful and immediate picture of greatness in God's kingdom! Jesus used many such props and visual aids in his teaching. For example, he used fish, coins, wine, dirt, mountains, a fig tree, and the temple as visual aids. When talking with Thomas after his resurrection, he even used his own body as a tool to inspire Thomas' faith.

Like Jesus, we have a plethora of items that we can use as visual aids in the classroom. For a listing of just some of the simple visual aids available to you, see the "Visual Aids" box on page 112. As you look through the list, consider how you might use each of those props to present or illustrate a biblical truth in your teaching. You'll be surprised at how many ideas immediately come to mind. Use them!

Visual Aids

audio tapes/ music	foil	paper	shoes
balloons	food coloring	paper clips	slides
Bibles	ice	paper plates	snacks
books	index cards	paper towels	soap
bread	keys	pencils	spices
candles	light bulbs	pens	stones
chalk/ chalkboard	magazines	phone books	string
coins	maps	pillows	sugar
colored paper	markers	plastic wrap	toilet paper
cookies	matches	potatoes	towels
cups	mirrors	puppets	trash bags
erasers	music	rubber bands	video tapes
file folders	name tags	rulers	watches
flashlights	newspaper	salt/pepper	water
flour	newsprint	scissors	wood
	overhead projectors	shaving cream	
		sheets	

Using Lecture, Discussion, and Debate the Way Jesus Did

In closing, let's review the main points we've covered:

1. Use lecture and discussion to reveal Jesus—not just your topic. (This is Principle 5.)

2. Never use lecture simply as a way to "dump information."

3. Use lecture and debate as a tool to demonstrate that you understand your students.

4. If your students don't think you understand them or where they're at, they won't listen to you.

5. Use all the tools at your disposal to get people directly involved in your lectures.

6. Use stories and visual aids to make your lectures and discussions memorable.

Lecture has often been slandered as a "dead" teaching tool in recent years. But as one educator, Stephen Brookfield, has noted, "for having expired so frequently, its corpse displays a remarkable liveliness."[7] The truth is that, if used effectively and for the right reasons, lecture, along with debate and discussion, can be powerful and effective tools to help us teach the way Jesus taught.

In the next chapter, we'll study what is arguably the most persuasive tool Jesus used as a teacher with his students—direct, real-life experiences—and we'll discover many practical ways we can incorporate experiential learning into the classroom setting.

[1] Thom and Joani Schultz, *Why Nobody Learns Much of Anything at Church: And How to Fix It* (Loveland, CO: Group Publishing, 1993), 190-191.

[2] Perry W. H. Shaw, "Jesus: Oriental Teacher Par Excellence," Christian Education Journal, Spring 1997, 91.

[3] B. Boylan, *What's Your Point?* (New York, NY: Warner Books, 1988), 80. Quoted in *Why Nobody Learns Much of Anything at Church: And How to Fix It,* 191.

[4] Schultz, *Why Nobody Learns Much of Anything at Church: And How to Fix It,* 195.

[5] Ibid., adapted from pp. 198-199.

[6] Mike and Amy Nappa, *Bore No More!* (Loveland, CO: Group Publishing, 1995), 76-78. Used by permission.

[7] Stephen D. Brookfield, The Skillful Teacher (San Francisco: Jossey-Bass, 1990), 69. Quoted in *Teaching as Jesus Taught,* 166.

Chapter 6
Learning Through Experience

"Jesus knew that the Father had put all things under his power,
and that he had come from God and was returning to God;
so he got up from the meal, took off his outer clothing,
and wrapped a towel around his waist.
After that, he poured water into a basin and
began to wash his disciples' feet,
drying them with the towel that was wrapped around him.
He came to Simon Peter, who said to him,
'Lord, are you going to wash my feet?'
Jesus replied, 'You do not realize now what I am doing,
but later you will understand.' "
—John 13:3-7

Looking back on my teenage years in church, I can clearly remember one elderly lady named Frances. She was a quiet, gentle woman, a little frail perhaps, but she came to church every Sunday, rain or shine, and sat in the second row on the left side of the center aisle. We never said much to each other, just the occasional "hello" or "good to see you today." But she was always smiling, which is probably why I remember her so clearly.

One Sunday in my seventeenth year, I went to church to discover that Frances was not there. I didn't really think much of it until the pastor got up and informed the congregation that Frances had suffered a heart attack and was presently in stable but serious condition at Seton hospital. The pastor related the story of how he had been called into the hospital late last night, not long after Frances was admitted. Most of her children and their families lived in the area, and they had arrived a short time earlier. They were all very worried about Frances. Some of them cried and held each other while they waited for the doctors to let them in to see her.

After almost an hour, the doctors gave them permission to visit her.

Upon entering her room and seeing her connected to so many tubes and wires, her two daughters immediately burst into tears. But Frances gently reached out her hand and smiled as she patted them both on the arm.

Then the pastor leaned down and asked, "How are you doing, Frances?"

"I am not worried," came the weak reply. "The Lord has taken me this far. And I know he will not leave me now."

After relating the story, the pastor looked intently at the congregation and said, "One thing I know. Frances did not suddenly grow that kind of faith in the ambulance ride to the hospital."

How do we grow that kind of faith? What is the most powerful tool that God uses in our lives to cause us to learn and change so that we are transformed, little by little, into the image of Christ?

The answer: experience. Experience forms the core of everything we learn. Think back to a life-changing lesson you have learned. Did you learn that lesson from something you heard or something you read? Or did you learn that lesson from something you experienced?

Personal experience forms the backbone of education. It is the furnace that tests what we think we know, to prove whether we really know it or not. And it is the gateway to new lessons that, once learned, can never be lost.

Using experience as a teaching tool wasn't just another element in Christ's teaching. It was the foundation and the final proving ground for everything Christ taught. Let me make that point again. *Teaching through purposeful, real-life experiences was the primary tool Jesus used to test and solidify learning in others.*

I realize that is a bold statement to make. What about his parables and sayings? What about his discourses and discussions? Don't these also form the backbone of his teaching? It's true that every tool Jesus used was important, effective, and worthy to be emulated. But all of the other tools Jesus used would have been incomplete if he had not guided his disciples through purposeful, real-life experiences to bring his teachings to life. As one saying puts it:

Tell me, and I'll forget.
Show me, and I may remember.
Involve me, and I'll understand.

Jesus understood this principle and used experiences to instruct, illustrate, test, and solidify what he wanted people to learn. In fact, Jesus made it clear that what he did—the way he taught—was simply a reflection of the way the Father teaches. Consider these Scriptures:

"Jesus gave them this answer: 'I tell you the truth, the Son can do nothing by himself; he can do only what he sees his Father doing, because whatever the Father does the Son also does' " (John 5:19).

"Jesus answered, 'My teaching is not my own. It comes from him who sent me. If anyone chooses to do God's will, he will find out whether my teaching comes from God or whether I speak on my own' " (John 7:16-17).

So how does the Father teach? Just look at the Old Testament. How did all the men and women of faith learn how to follow God? Through his voice, certainly. But as with Jesus, the Father's teaching was solidified, amplified, or even introduced through experience.

The Bible, from cover to cover, details God's use of active learning. Abraham actively demonstrated the depth of his faith by raising his knife over Isaac (Genesis 22:1-13). Jonah learned about his inability to hide from God only after spending a little time in a fish's belly (Jonah 2:1-10)."[1]

And to this list we could add many more:
• Jacob learned about his own need for God by wrestling with an angel (Genesis 32:22-32).
• Moses learned about the nature of God through a burning bush (Exodus 3:1-6).
• The Israelites learned about trusting God by living in a desert for forty years (Exodus, Leviticus, Numbers, and Deuteronomy).
• Joshua learned about the power of faith in God by tumbling the walls of Jericho without lifting a sword (Joshua 6:1-27).
• David learned about the cost of sin by losing his son (2 Samuel 12:12-20).

And the list goes on. Time and again, God used real-life experiences to teach, test, and solidify the lessons he wanted his people to understand. Sometimes God would reveal the truth through his words, then prove it through experience. For example, he did this with Moses before leading him to confront Pharaoh. Other times he would step into the middle of an experience, revealing the point of the lesson as the experience continued. He did this with Shadrach, Meshach, and Abednego as they stood in the midst of the furnace. And other times he would speak after an experience had ended, to shed light on what had happened so that learning could occur. He did this with Abraham after he had offered his son Isaac on Mount Moriah.

Although how and where and when God speaks varies from situation to situation, the use of real-life experiences as a teaching tool is consistent throughout all of God's teaching in the Old Testament.

As a teacher, Jesus followed in his Father's footsteps. He taught the way the Father teaches, using real-life experiences in combination with his other teaching methods to instruct, test, and solidify learning in his followers.

The evidence that Jesus used experience continues today through the Holy Spirit. In John 14:26, Jesus says, "But the Counselor, the Holy Spirit, whom the Father will send in my name, will teach you all things and will remind you of everything I have said to you." In verse 16 of this same chapter, Jesus describes the Holy Spirit by using the Greek word *allos,* which means "another of the same sort."[2] So Jesus seems to be telling his disciples—and us—that the Holy Spirit will be a teacher of the same sort as he is. Paul even referred to the Holy Spirit as "the Spirit of Christ" (Romans 8:9), indicating that it is, in fact, the Spirit of Jesus who lives within us and teaches us.

Consider your own walk with God. How does the Holy Spirit teach you? Certainly, God uses his Word to reveal truth to our hearts. He also uses the words of others—even (I hope and pray) words written in a book like this one. But how is that truth illuminated, tested, and solidified within us? Through real-life experiences.

How many times has a verse of Scripture or a biblical truth come to life in your heart after you've gone through an experience? And in those times, you say to yourself in amazement, "I must've read that verse a thousand times, but it has never hit home until now!"

Or how many times has the Holy Spirit found a point of resistance in your heart and used experiences to expose it—again and again, if necessary? Each time we repent, we find ourselves saying, "How many times will I have to go through this before I learn?"

God—the Father, the Son, and the Holy Spirit—uses purposeful, real-life experiences as the classroom, the testing lab, and the proving ground for all of his teaching. As teachers who want to follow in his steps, we must also learn to use real-life experiences as the foundation and core of all that we teach our students.

Principle 6
Teach, test, and solidify learning through real-life experiences.

At first glance, this principle may sound impossible to accomplish. After all, Jesus traveled side by side with his disciples for three years. Real-life experiences were a part of their daily routine. But our circumstances are different. We don't live with our students, and outside of a few socials or field trips, we don't spend our days experiencing life side by side. So how can we guide students through real-life experiences within the confines of a classroom?

To be honest, sometimes we can't. Sometimes guiding students through purposeful, real-life experiences means getting out of the classroom and venturing together into the world. But there are also many ways we can use experiences to teach without ever leaving the building. To discover how this can be done, let's first examine a few of the experiences Jesus used to teach his disciples. Then we'll consider how we can translate each one into the modern classroom.

How Jesus Used Experiences to Teach

Jesus used three categories of learning experiences to teach his disciples: teachable moments; direct, purposeful adventures; and creative, planned experiences. We'll examine these in the order of their frequency in Jesus' ministry.

Teachable Moments

In Jesus' teaching ministry, teachable moments occurred any time Jesus drew a lesson from an unplanned, real-life experience that happened to himself or his disciples. Jesus used teachable moments more often than any other experiential teaching tool. To discover how he used them, let's consider two examples.

The first is described in Matthew 14:22-33.

Immediately Jesus made the disciples get into the boat and go on ahead of him to the other side, while he dismissed the crowd. After he had dismissed them, he went up on a mountainside by himself to pray. When evening came, he was there alone, but the boat was already a considerable distance from land, buffeted by the waves because the wind was against it.

During the fourth watch of the night Jesus went out to them, walking on the lake. When the disciples saw him walking on the lake, they were terrified. "It's a ghost," they said, and cried out in fear.

But Jesus immediately said to them: "Take courage! It is I. Don't be afraid."

"Lord, if it's you," Peter replied, "tell me to come to you on the water."

"Come," he said.

Then Peter got down out of the boat, walked on the water and came toward Jesus. But when he saw the wind, he was afraid and, beginning to sink, cried out, "Lord, save me!"

Immediately Jesus reached out his hand and caught him. "You of little faith," he said, "why did you doubt?"

And when they climbed into the boat, the wind died down. Then those who were in the boat worshiped him, saying, "Truly you are the Son of God."

What a beautiful picture of what it means to walk in faith in the middle of turbulent circumstances! As followers of Christ, we can walk through difficult and even impossible situations simply by keeping our eyes on Jesus and walking toward him. But by allowing ourselves to be distracted by fearful circumstances, we can lose sight of Jesus and lose our connection with his power and guidance in our lives. Essentially, it's the same lesson Jesus taught in the Parable of the Sower, when he talked about the seed that was choked out by the weeds, which are the worries and cares of this world.

What if you had been in Peter's place? Or what if you had been one of the disciples who stayed in the boat? Just think of the impact this experience had on teaching the disciples about real faith!

And what made it possible? The disciples' reaction to seeing Jesus walk on water, and Peter's request, presented a teachable moment that Jesus took as an opportunity to teach this powerful lesson about faith.

But wait a minute? Wasn't this planned? Didn't Jesus plot how he was going to shock the disciples by walking on the water and use it as an example of faith? The answer is most likely "no." We know that because of the way Mark describes the encounter in Mark 6:48-50.

> He [Jesus] saw the disciples straining at the oars, because the wind was against them. About the fourth watch of the night he went out to them, walking on the lake. *He was about to pass by them,* but when they saw him walking on the lake, they thought he was a ghost. They cried out, because they all saw him and were terrified. (author emphasis)

Based on the text, Jesus never intended to get into the boat at all. But when his disciples reacted to seeing him, and Peter made his request, Jesus saw a teachable moment that he could use to impact his disciples. And he took it.

Here are just a few other examples of teachable moments Jesus used to drive home important lessons to his disciples. Read through each of these to see if you can discover how you might recognize and use teachable moments more effectively in your own teaching.

- Jesus heals a paralytic—Matthew 9:1-8
- Jesus calms the storm—Mark 4:35-41
- Jesus heals a boy with an evil spirit—Mark 9:14-29
- Jesus is anointed by a woman—Luke 7:36-50
- Jesus teaches Martha—Luke 10:38-42
- Jesus raises Lazarus from the dead—John 11:1-44

As diverse as these experiences are, there is a consistent pattern in the way Jesus recognized and used teachable moments to inspire learning. I'll list them here as directives we can follow to use teachable moments in our own classrooms:

1. Recognize that a teachable moment occurs any time circumstances provoke an emotional response in students. In every Scripture listed above, the students' emotions were engaged by the circumstance, and that emotional connection is what can lead to learning. Often (but not always) such emotional responses came as a result of circumstances that were either unexpected or unwanted. However they came, it was in these emotionally-charged moments that Jesus saw the opportunity for learning.

Now please don't misunderstand what I'm saying. I do not mean to say that learning cannot occur on a purely intellectual level. As we've pointed out in Jesus' use of parables, sayings, lectures, and discussions, provoking people to intellectually examine truth is essential to true learning.

But, when it comes to learning through *experience,* it is usually our emotional reaction, more than our intellectual response, that provokes us to learn. How did Peter learn his important lesson about faith? By experiencing fear on the water. How did the disciples learn about the role of prayer in spiritual warfare? By experiencing frustration at their inability to help the boy with the evil spirit.

The implications for us as teachers are enormous. Any time an experience happens in which emotions are engaged, a teachable moment is at hand. Every time a child cries, gets angry, or misbehaves, it's a teachable moment. Every time the adults in your class get into an uncomfortable debate or react emotionally to some event in the news, it's a teachable moment. The truth is that teachable moments happen all the time, all around us.

For example, Joani Schultz tells the story of one teachable moment that presented itself as she was leading a workshop on children's ministry. Joani was sharing with the participants the importance of letting kids talk openly and share their opinions during a Bible lesson. Such open communication, said Joani, helps kids learn more effectively, and provides an effective barometer for teachers to know whether kids are actually learning. After workshop participants talked in pair-shares, a woman from the crowd stood up and said, "I don't see why children should be allowed to talk when the lesson is being presented. I've been through classes where teachers did nothing but lecture, and the children learned just fine that way."

The teachable moment had arrived. The woman obviously had an emotional response to Joani's comments. And her vocal objections probably produced an emotional response in the other participants. It was the perfect time to drive the lesson home.

Unfortunately, in this situation, Joani let the teachable moment slip by. In retrospect, she says she should have responded by saying: "Thank you so much for your observations and for illustrating my point. You see, if you did not have the freedom to speak up, I might have simply continued talking about this issue and assumed that every one of you understood and agreed with what I was saying. But because you felt the freedom to share, I understand more about where you stand and what we're all learning. You have beautifully illustrated why students should be talking in our classrooms."

If we know how to recognize them, we can use teachable moments to inspire powerful learning in our students.

Teacher's Corner: Teachable Moments

Most of us have heard about "teachable moments" in the classroom. But what exactly are they, and how can we recognize them when they come?

A teachable moment occurs any time your students encounter a situation that holds a lesson that they can learn. Sometimes the lesson is obvious and requires little effort from you to make it clear. Other times the lesson may be "hidden," and you need to draw it out so students can see it and learn from it. Although teachable moments come in many forms, here are a few clues to help you recognize and utilize teachable moments in your classroom.

• A teachable moment can occur whenever something captures your students' attention. Are your students curious about a recent news event? Are they concerned about some issue troubling your church or some problem they're facing at home? Then you can use their curiosity and interest to spark learning—by connecting the issue back to God. For example, you could ask, "How do you think God feels about that issue?" "What do you think Jesus would say about this issue if he were here in the flesh today?" "How do you think God wants you to respond to this situation?"

• A teachable moment can occur whenever students are confused or perplexed. Confusion often motivates students to seek answers. When you sense that students are confused about something—whether it's a question about the Bible or a question about life—you can inspire learning by encouraging students to seek God for the answers. For example, if students are confused about the ethical debate surrounding abortion, use their confusion as a launching point for a Bible study on that issue. The answers they find will not only help them settle their minds, but will also train them to seek God for answers to other confusing issues they may encounter.

• Teachable moments can occur whenever a student expresses a need. Is one of your students in financial trouble? Seize the teachable moment by organizing a whole-class fund-raiser or taking up an offering. Is one of your students sick? Take the class to visit him or her and pray for healing. Teachable moments like these occur all the time, and taking simple steps to respond to people's needs can help students learn about their faith in ways that have a lasting impact on their lives.

• Teachable moments can occur whenever class members express appreciation for one another. Personal, direct affirmation of a student's qualities or behavior can inspire students to learn from each other's example, and can provide real-life illustrations of what it means to live out the Bible's commands. For example, does one of your students typically demonstrate compassion toward others in the classroom? When you see it, praise it. Doing this will not only encourage the student you praise, but will also help the rest of the class recognize that quality and develop it in their own lives.

2. Don't squelch a teachable moment just because it's uncomfortable. Many times, teachable moments can be very uncomfortable. Why do you suppose, for example, that when Jesus heard that Lazarus was near death, he decided to stay where he was another three days instead of going to his friend's side? Because he saw that a powerful teachable moment could come out of the horrible anxiety Mary and Martha must have felt as they waited those three days and watched their brother die. To some of us, Jesus' choice may even sound cruel, but he understood that the eternal lesson Mary and Martha would learn would be more than worth the painful uneasiness they felt as they waited for Jesus.

Many times, we teachers react to uncomfortable situations in our classrooms by trying to immediately "fix" the problem. If two kids are arguing, we separate them. If two adults heatedly disagree about an issue, we change the subject. If someone in our youth class becomes emotional and starts to cry over the pain in his or her life, we hand the person a tissue and say, "Don't cry." Why? Probably because we're uncomfortable, and we're worried that other people might be uncomfortable too. Unfortunately, we're missing many powerful teachable moments because we value our comfort more than learning.

Jesus didn't squelch circumstances just because they were uncomfortable. And neither should we.

Teacher's Corner: "Uncomfortable" or "Inappropriate"?

When we say that we shouldn't squelch teachable moments just because they're uncomfortable, we don't mean to imply that any teacher should permit behavior or situations that are inappropriate or wrong. Two children arguing may be uncomfortable; two children hitting each other is certainly inappropriate and should be stopped immediately. Likewise, it may be uncomfortable for two adults to argue over an issue. But it becomes inappropriate if those adults begin to slander each other on a personal level.

In your classroom, use discernment in determining whether a situation is simply uncomfortable or inappropriate.

3. Rather than force the point, let the lesson present itself. When Jesus saw Martha running around the house in a frenzy while Mary sat at his feet, he did not go and confront Martha on her wrong attitude. Instead, he let the situation have its effect, and waited for Martha herself to instigate the learning. The same pattern is true in every Scripture listed earlier in the chapter. Jesus did not initiate the lesson, but rather waited until his disciples reacted verbally to the circumstance, either with a question, with a comment, or, in the case of Jesus walking on water, with an exclamation. Only then did Jesus step in to teach.

> *"Active learning is an adventure! And if we really believe that, it means that as a teacher, you cannot force anybody to get out of the experience what you think they should get out of it—if it truly is an active-learning experience."*
>
> —Joani Schultz

Too often in our teaching, we're so anxious for our students to "get the point" that we don't allow them the opportunity to experience the full lesson for themselves before we drive the point home. Before jumping into a teachable moment, wait for your students to respond. And if you must say something, limit yourself to questions like these:

- What's your reaction to this circumstance?
- What do you think about what's happened here?
- How do you feel about this situation?

Of course, for us as modern teachers, teachable moments may be harder to come by. As we've already stated, unlike Jesus and his disciples, we don't live side by side with our students on a daily basis. Even so, teachable moments do frequently happen in the classroom. And we can take advantage of them if we can learn to recognize and utilize them when they occur.

Direct, Purposeful Adventures

A direct, purposeful adventure is basically a planned encounter between your students and the real world. Jesus used this type of experience typically as a way to test and solidify the lessons he taught his disciples, as well as a way for them to gain new insights on their own.

Two of the best-known examples of this teaching tool in Scripture can be found in Luke 9:1-6 (the sending of the Twelve) and Luke 10:1-12, 16-20 (the sending of the seventy-two). Let's take a look at these two experiences.

When Jesus had called the Twelve together, he gave them power and authority to drive out all demons and to cure diseases, and he sent them out to preach the kingdom of God and to heal the sick. He told them: "Take nothing for the journey—no staff, no bag, no bread, no money, no extra tunic. Whatever house you enter, stay there until you leave that town. If people do not welcome you, shake the dust off your feet when you leave their town, as a testimony against them." So they set out and went from village to village, preaching the gospel and healing people everywhere (Luke 9:1-6).

After this the Lord appointed seventy-two others and sent them two by two ahead of him to every town and place where he was about to go. He told them, "The harvest is plentiful, but the workers are few. Ask the Lord of the harvest, therefore, to send out workers into his harvest field. Go! I am sending you out like lambs among wolves. Do not take a purse or bag or sandals; and do not greet anyone on the road.

"When you enter a town and are welcomed, eat what is set before you. Heal the sick who are there and tell them, 'The kingdom of God is near you.' But when you enter a town and are not welcomed, go into its streets and say, 'Even the dust of your town that sticks to our feet we wipe off against you. Yet be sure of this: The kingdom of God is near.' I tell you, it will be more bearable on that day for Sodom than for that town. He who listens to you listens to me; he who rejects you rejects me; but he who rejects me rejects him who sent me."

The seventy-two returned with joy and said, "Lord, even the demons submit to us in your name."

He replied, "I saw Satan fall like lightning from heaven. I have given you authority to trample on snakes and scorpions and to overcome all the power of the enemy; nothing will harm you. However do not rejoice that the spirits submit to you, but rejoice that your names are written in heaven" (Luke 10:1-4, 8-12, 16-20).

Just like these experiences, modern-day purposeful experiences can be situations that involve students interacting with people for the purpose of demonstrating their faith—by serving them, meeting their needs, and telling them about Christ. These purposeful experiences include just about anything we now call "service projects." They might include:

- visiting people in nursing homes,
- going to hospitals to pray for the sick,
- repairing or refurbishing low-income homes,
- feeding or serving the homeless,
- working as a tutor,
- volunteering in a crisis counseling center,
- working with troubled youth,
- doing yardwork or other repairs for elderly couples,
- working as a volunteer in an after-school program,
- going on short-term mission trips (local or overseas), or
- going door-to-door to share faith.

This list goes on. Even though there are many diverse activities to choose from, some elements are common to all direct, purposeful experiences—including the ones Jesus did with his disciples. You can use these common characteristics as guidelines to help you design these types of adventures for your students.

1. They are planned. Unlike teachable moments, direct, purposeful adventures are strategically planned encounters between your students and the real world.

2. They focus on sharing faith. That doesn't mean that every service project must be overtly evangelistic. But it does mean that any direct, purposeful experience should be primarily motivated by and be an obvious expression of our faith in Jesus. So whether we're feeding the homeless, painting a house, or playing basketball with inner city kids, our goal in every situation should be clear: to demonstrate our faith in Christ through our actions and words.

3. They expose Christians to the real world. In both of the biblical accounts on page 125, Jesus did not go with his disciples to watch over the experience. Instead, after giving clear instructions, he sent them out on their own. That doesn't mean we should not participate with our students when they dive into a direct, purposeful experience, but we

must be willing to let our students encounter the real world on their own, and not try to shield them from unpleasant realities or from making mistakes in the midst of unfamiliar circumstances.

4. They involve risk. Jesus clearly explained to his disciples that he was sending them into a risky situation, where they would be "like lambs among wolves." Some of the people they encountered would reject them and their message. Jesus did not try to shield them from this risk, but rather gave clear instructions on how they should respond in each situation. In the same way, any direct, purposeful experience that we plan should involve genuine risk for our students. That's because risk creates an environment in which learning can thrive. Where there is no risk, there is no challenge. Where there is no challenge, there is no learning.

That doesn't mean a learning experience has to be terrifying to be effective. For example, taking your class to visit people in a nursing home isn't life-threatening, but it may be an effective first step toward sharing faith in a risky environment. After an experience like that, maybe your students will be ready to tackle something even more risky, such as praying for the sick in a hospital or visiting inmates at the local prison.

Essentially, direct, purposeful experiences are simply planned teachable moments. Consequently, once the experience begins, you should treat it as any other teachable moment. During (or following) the experience, look for your students' emotional reactions to the event. Wait for them to initiate the learning by telling you what they feel. Then you can use their reactions as a point of learning that will have a permanent impact on their lives.

Notice that's exactly what Jesus did when the seventy-two returned from their journey. Upon their return, the disciples spoke first, expressing to Jesus their joy over being able to overthrow demonic forces. And Jesus used their response as a point of learning, encouraging their enthusiasm while at the same time teaching them about the importance of maintaining a humble

> *"We've all done things that we thought were failures, and later found out that some people were really moved or touched by what happened. We just have to accept that we can't see what's happening inside a person, and we don't always know how the Holy Spirit may be working through an experience."*
>
> —Joani Schultz

attitude in the midst of spiritual warfare.

But what if you don't know what kind of lesson you should pull from the experience? What if the experience was a total disaster, or your students were simply bored by the whole thing? What sort of life-changing lesson can you pull from something like that?

Don't worry. You don't have to have all the answers. Even if you can't see any lesson springing from a particular experience, God can. And even if you don't draw out any life-changing lessons for your students, God will. Remember Principle 3?

Principle 3
Believe that if they are teachable, they will learn.

Teaching through experience is a risky act of faith—for you and your students. Some students involved in the experience might not get the lesson *you* want them to learn. But as long as you are faithful to expose your students to real-life experiences, the Holy Spirit will see to it that those who are teachable will gain the lessons *God* wants them to learn. And if that happens, your teaching will be a success.

Creative, Planned Experiences

A planned experience occurs any time you design a creative activity, event, or situation that evokes an emotional response in your students. These types of experiences differ from direct, purposeful adventures in that they typically "simulate" something in real life, but don't *usually* involve a direct encounter with the real world (though sometimes they do). For example, role-plays, learning games, and simulation games all fall within this category.

Two occasions when Jesus used these types of creative, planned experiences to inspire learning in his disciples can be found in John 2:13-22 and in John 13:3-17. As you read through these planned experiences, notice how the experiences evoked different emotions in different people.

"In our approach to education, kids need to encounter the real God, not just hear about God...we need to create situations where they're face to face with God."

—Christine Yount

When it was almost time for the Jewish Passover, Jesus went up to Jerusalem. In the temple courts he found men selling cattle, sheep and doves, and others sitting at tables exchanging money. So he made a whip out of cords, and drove all from the temple area, both sheep and cattle; he scattered the coins of the money changers and overturned their tables. To those who sold doves he said, "Get these out of here! How dare you turn my Father's house into a market!"

His disciples remembered that it is written: "Zeal for your house will consume me."

Then the Jews demanded of him, "What miraculous sign can you show us to prove your authority to do all this?"

Jesus answered them, "Destroy this temple, and I will raise it again in three days."

The Jews replied, "It has taken forty-six years to build this temple, and you are going to raise it in three days?" But the temple he had spoken of was his body. After he was raised from the dead, his disciples recalled what he had said. Then they believed the Scripture and the words that Jesus had spoken (John 2:13-22).

Jesus knew that the Father had put all things under his power, and that he had come from God and was returning to God; so he got up from the meal, took off his outer clothing, and wrapped a towel around his waist. After that, he poured water into a basin and began to wash his disciples' feet, drying them with the towel that was wrapped around him.

He came to Simon Peter, who said to him, "Lord, are you going to wash my feet?"

Jesus replied, "You do not realize now what I am doing, but later you will understand."

"No," said Peter, "you shall never wash my feet."

Jesus answered, "Unless I wash you, you have no part with me."

"Then, Lord," Simon Peter replied, "not just my feet but my hands and my head as well!"

Jesus answered, "A person who has had a bath needs only to wash his feet; his whole body is clean. And you are clean, though not every one of you." For he knew who was going to betray him, and that was why he said not every one was clean.

When he had finished washing their feet, he put on his clothes and returned to his place. "Do you understand what I have done for you?" he asked them. "You call me 'Teacher' and 'Lord,' and rightly so, for that is what I am. Now that I, your Lord and Teacher, have washed your feet, you also should wash one another's feet. I have set you an example that you should do as I have done for you. I tell you the truth, no servant is greater than his master, nor is a messenger greater than the one who sent him. Now that you know these things, you will be blessed if you do them" (John 13:3-17).

Each of these is an example of a different type of learning experience. In the first, the disciples and the Jews were emotionally caught up in the experience of watching Jesus clear the temple, even though they weren't physically involved. In the second, the disciples were both physically and emotionally engaged in the action. Both situations, however, evoked a variety of responses in either the disciples or the Jews, producing a variety of results. The experiences caused some participants to learn the lesson on the spot. Others learned the lesson over time. And a few never learned the lesson at all. Let's take a look at each of these results to see how it applies to us as experiential teachers today.

1. In experiential learning, some students understand the lesson on the spot. When Jesus cleared the temple, his disciples stood by and watched as their rabbi tore the place apart in what might have seemed like a rage. What were they feeling as they watched him do this? Embarrassed? Nervous about how people would react? And what lessons could they gain from the experience?

We know something about how the disciples responded because of John's comment in verse 17. As they watched Jesus clear the temple, John writes: "His disciples remembered that it is written: 'Zeal for your house will consume me.' " So we can surmise that, at least to a degree, the disciples responded to Jesus' actions with faith, so that the experience immediately strengthened their belief in Jesus as the Messiah. They learned a lesson on the spot.

The same response can happen in our classrooms today. After taking students through an experience, we will find that some of them will be able to draw immediate lessons to apply to their lives. In some cases, this is accomplished through debriefing the experience—by asking questions or helping students process the event. In other cases (as with the disciples in the first passage), the learning can take place spontaneously, with no debriefing at all.

2. In experiential learning, most students understand the lesson over time. In John 13:7, Jesus told his disciples, "You do not realize now what I am doing, but later you will understand." In this statement, Jesus reveals his understanding of a fundamental truth about learning from experience. He knew that most lessons gained from experience don't hit us all at once. Instead, they are gleaned over time, as we process what has happened. Understanding this aspect of experiential learning is one of the keys to releasing the real power of this educational tool. We need to give students time to discover experiential lessons for themselves.

In modern education, we teachers often feel compelled to "drive the point home" immediately for our students. We don't feel successful until we've drawn the conclusion, revealed the answer, or shared the moral of the story. But, when it comes to experiential learning, Jesus was willing to wait until the experience was over before he revealed the lesson. He understood that for most people, learning from an experience can take time.

> *"Judas is the key example of someone 'not getting it.' But the other disciples didn't get it either, and yet, somewhere down the line, they really get it. I mean, they get it in an incredible way. That's amazing to me."*
>
> —Rick Lawrence

And so rather than force the point or lesson upon them, Jesus let the experience happen before he revealed the point he wanted to convey.

3. In experiential learning, a few students will never understand the lesson at all. When the Jews watched Jesus clear the temple, they got emotionally involved and even discussed the experience with Jesus afterward. But they never gained the insights about Christ that the disciples did. In the same way, even though Judas allowed Jesus to wash his feet, he never understood the same lesson Peter gained.

Why didn't they learn? Were the experiences flawed in some way? No. Was Jesus an ineffective teacher with these people? Of course not. Then why didn't they get it?

Principle 1
Realize that people cannot understand truth unless God enables them.

In experiential learning, as with parables, lectures, and discussions, no learning can happen unless people's hearts are teachable and open to God. Experiential learning is good. In fact, it's essential for teachers who want to teach as Jesus did. But some people will not learn from experience, even if the lessons are laid out plainly before them. Even though Jesus knew this, he didn't let that fact stop him from using experiential learning as a teaching tool. And neither should we.

Teacher's Corner: A Word About Debriefing

As we've already noted, when Jesus encountered teachable moments, he usually let the students instigate the learning process by waiting for them to share their reactions to the experience or event. Then he used their responses as a launching point to guide them toward a new discovery or lesson.

In modern teaching, we can accomplish the same goal by asking students a few simple questions after any learning experience. These questions are not designed to make a point; rather, their goal is to help students process their own reactions to the experience and begin to gain lessons from it that they can apply to their lives.

Here are a few questions you can use to help your students process any experience you take them through. The questions are divided into three sections:

1. Reflection—Questions that help students process their feelings:

● What's your reaction to this experience?

● How did you feel during this experience?

● How do you feel about what just happened? Explain.

2. Interpretation—Questions that help students make a connection between this experience and a biblical principle:

● What does this experience mean to you?

● What does this experience tell you about life? about God? about yourself?

● What are some immediate lessons you can gain from this experience?

3. Application—Questions that help students think about how this experience might impact their lives:

● How might this experience change the way you think?

- How might this experience change the way you live?
- If you were to give someone any advice about life based on this experience, what would you say?

Reasons Christian Teachers Refuse to Use Experiential Learning

Jesus used real-life experiences to teach, test, and solidify learning in students' lives. In fact, real-life experiences formed the foundation of his approach to teaching. And yet many Christian teachers are afraid to use experiences as a teaching tool with students. Why? Here are a few common reasons:

1. Experiential learning is too risky— Some people won't "get it." Actually, if the research is true, then teaching through experience is the *least* risky way to get a truth across to your students. That's because we remember about 90 percent of what we experience firsthand, as opposed to only 10 percent of what we hear in a lecture. In fact, the sense of risk we feel doesn't really revolve around whether students will learn anything. (Research indicates that they will.) The real risk revolves around whether they will learn *what we want them to learn*. But that's a risk that is definitely worth taking. Thom and Joani Schultz state it this way:

> *"When Jesus fed the five thousand, there were lots of people in lots of different places all experiencing the same thing, but each of them had to interpret it where they were at. So, in our context, when we ask, 'Should we do this experience?' because we're worried that people aren't ready for it; well, yes, they are ready for it! Jesus did it with five thousand!"*
>
> —Joani Schultz

Teachers still fret about active learning. "What if they don't get the point I'm trying to get across?" Well, maybe they'll learn something *better* than the teacher intended. Active learning allows students to learn different truths from the same experience. Can we not trust the Holy Spirit to guide our learners?[3]

Trusting the Holy Spirit not only means that students may glean lessons we never intended, but also that they may take a long time to glean the lessons we do intend. We can't expect experiential lessons to always make sense to our students right away. Sometimes people have to go through experiences more than once before they learn what God is trying to teach them.

There's a story about two hunters who flew into a remote part of Canada to go elk hunting. Their hunt was a great success, and by the end of their trip they had bagged six elk. So when their pilot returned to pick them up, they excitedly told him all about their adventure. But when the pilot saw that they had six elk, he frowned and told them the plane could carry out only four.

"But the plane that carried us out last year was exactly like this one," the hunters protested. "The horsepower was the same, the weather was similar, and we had six elk then, too."

Upon hearing this, the pilot reluctantly agreed to carry out all the elk. They loaded up and took off. But the pilot quickly realized that because of the extra weight, there wasn't enough power to climb out of the valley. Just minutes after taking off, the plane crashed. As they stumbled from the wreckage, one hunter asked the other if he knew where they were.

"Well, I'm not sure," replied the second, "but I think we're only about two miles from where we crashed last year."[4]

Don't be surprised if your students don't seem to learn anything from a teaching experience right away. If they are teachable, they will learn in time. As one saying puts it, "Don't underestimate the importance of experience. It'll help you recognize a mistake when you make it again."[5]

2. Experiential learning is too unpredictable—I can't control what students learn. Some teachers place great confidence in dull workbooks and "information dump" lectures, mostly because these techniques give the illusion of thoroughness in teaching. After all, all the information is right there, laid out for the students to absorb. The only problem is that students often fail to absorb much of anything with these techniques.

The truth is, experiential learning *is* unpredictable. As teachers, we cannot easily control what students will learn. But that lack of control is exactly what makes experiential learning so effective, because it allows room for God to teach different lessons to different people, each according to their needs.

3. Experiential learning wastes the teacher's wisdom—All students do is discuss their reactions. Nothing could be further from the truth. As a teacher, your wisdom is essential for experiential learning to be effective.

How? By wisely choosing and guiding students into experiences that God can use to powerfully impact their lives. And after the experience is over, your wisdom and insight about the event can also be essential to helping students learn powerful lessons that will impact them for a lifetime.

4. Experiential learning isn't a trustworthy technique—Some experiences fail to teach anything. Again, not true. The beauty of experiential learning is that genuine learning can take place regardless of the outcome of the experience. Jesus taught his disciples about the importance of following his commands and "abiding" in him in order to have life (John 15). Soon after that, however, Peter failed to follow Jesus' instructions and actually denied he even knew Jesus at all. Peter's experience at following Christ was a failure by almost all accounts.

But Jesus did not leave it there. In John 21:15-19, Jesus "debriefs" the experience with Peter and guides him to discover a powerful lesson about God's forgiveness. So great learning can occur even in what seems to be the worst failures.

To teach the way Jesus taught, we must use all types of experiential learning—teachable moments; direct, purposeful adventures; and creative, planned experiences—as the foundation and backbone of all the teaching we do with students. For some of us, that may mean rethinking what we do in education, and redirecting our efforts to include experiential learning in a way that emulates Jesus' teaching style more fully. For others, only a few minor adjustments in our teaching may be necessary. But all of us can choose to see these sorts of changes as a learning experience of our own. And the lessons we learn from it may have a life-changing impact on us as well as our students.

[1] Thom and Joani Schultz, *Do It! Active Learning In Youth Ministry* (Loveland, CO: Group Publishing, 1989), 20.

[2] Vine's Expository Dictionary of Biblical Words, ed. by W.E. Vine, Merrill F. Unger, and William White, Jr. (Nashville, TN: Thomas Nelson Publishers, 1985), 29.

[3] Schultz, *Why Nobody Learns Much of Anything at Church: And How to Fix It,* 120.

[4] Adapted from "Help From Experience" in *Illustrations Unlimited,* ed. by James S. Hewett (Wheaton, IL: Tyndale House Publishers, 1988), 184. Used by permission. All rights reserved.

[5] *Illustrations Unlimited,* ed. by James S. Hewett, 184. Used by permission. All rights reserved.

Chapter 7
Asking the Right Questions

"While the Pharisees were gathered together, Jesus asked them,
'What do you think about the Christ? Whose son is he?'
'The son of David,' they replied.
He said to them, 'How is it then that David,
speaking by the Spirit, calls him "Lord"? For he says,
"The Lord said to my Lord: Sit at my right hand
until I put your enemies under your feet."
If then David calls him "Lord," how can he be his son?'
No one could say a word in reply, and from that day on no one dared
to ask him any more questions."
—Matthew 22:41-46

Have you ever asked your students a question to intentionally dumbfound them?

Have you ever asked a question that you never intended students to answer?

Have you ever asked a question to expose wrong thinking, test your students' faith, or confront sin in their lives?

If you have, then you know something about how Jesus used questions in his teaching.

Jesus' use of questions was anything but typical. By at least one theologian's account, Jesus asked more than three hundred questions[1]—directed to individuals, his disciples, his adversaries, or the crowds—and every one of them hit its target in a way that challenged, amazed, and even shocked his listeners.

How would *you* respond if Jesus had asked you questions like these?

"If you love those who love you, what reward will you get?"   Matthew 5:46a

"Who of you by worrying can add a single hour to his life?"   Matthew 6:27

"Why do you look at the speck of sawdust in your brother's eye and pay no attention to the plank in your own eye?"	Matthew 7:3
"You of little faith, why are you so afraid?"	Matthew 8:26a
"Why do you entertain evil thoughts in your hearts?"	Matthew 9:4
"And why do you break the command of God for the sake of your tradition?"	Matthew 15:3
"Judas, are you betraying the Son of Man with a kiss?"	Luke 22:48

Pretty exposing questions, aren't they? Reading through this list, you can probably tell that many of the questions Jesus asked were never intended to be answered. In fact, although Jesus did use questions to elicit information, very often he chose to ask questions that were largely "unanswerable"—to expose sin, reveal truth, or challenge people to think. He used questions boldly, skillfully constructing them to powerfully address the need of the moment. An educator once wrote, "In the skillful use of the question more than anything else lies the fine art of teaching; for in such use we have the guide to clear and vivid ideas, the quick spur to imagination, the stimulus to thought, the incentive to action."[2]

Just a quick scan through Jesus' questions will tell you: He understood the educational power that comes from asking the right questions at the right moment in the right way. He was the most effective "questioner" who has ever lived. As Roy B. Zuck observed:

> Jesus asked clear, direct, purposeful questions that made his teaching stimulating, spirited, and soul-searching. His queries aroused interest, provoked thought, requested information, elicited response, clarified issues, applied truth, and silenced critics.[3]

Who would've thought a question could do all that! By studying the types of questions Jesus' used and examining why he used them, we can discover several key principles to using questions more effectively in our own teaching. And with those new tools in hand, we can learn to follow God's Spirit in such a way that the questions we ask will not only challenge students to think, but potentially impact the course of their lives.

"Jesus never asks questions like the questions in your high school Sunday school class."

—Thom Schultz

The Questions Jesus Asked

I've always had a curious hatred for the game show *Jeopardy*. It's the only game show I know of that has the ability to make so many people feel so stupid in so short a time. Just watching these Ph.D. students, professors, and scientists battle for superiority of knowledge about "Peruvian Inventors" or "Ocean Plant Life" could make just about any reasonably intelligent viewer feel like an idiot. And what is the point of the answers—which, for reasons almost no one understands, are always in the form of a question? To test the players' wisdom about life? To gauge their understanding about relationships, love, and eternity—the things that really matter? No. The only purpose is to test their knowledge of facts. That's it.

The show may gain the contestants some money if they win, but other than that, I feel like it's largely a waste of my time. Few people can learn any valuable lessons about life if they're asked *only* to spout facts and figures.

Isn't it curious, then, that most educators today use questions primarily for that reason—to get students to spout facts? "What's the square root of 25?" "Who shot Abraham Lincoln?" "Where was Jesus born?" One study showed that 60 percent of teachers' questions require kids to spout facts, and another 20 percent deal with procedural matters. That means that only one out of five questions teachers ask actually provoke students to think.[4] In another more recent study, the results were even worse. That study found that fewer than 1 percent of teachers' questions actually inspired kids to think.[5]

Jesus did sometimes ask questions to elicit factual information. But far more often, he used questions to accomplish entirely different, yet much more powerful goals. Let's take a look at each of the ways Jesus used questions, and explore how we can translate his questioning techniques into our classrooms today.

1. Jesus used questions to initiate a conversation. Like many teachers today, Jesus sometimes used questions as a way to start a conversation. For example, to open a conversation with the woman at the well, Jesus asked her, "Will you give me a drink?" (John 4:7). Likewise, when Jesus wanted to talk with the disciples on the road to Emmaus, he asked them, "What are you discussing together as you walk along?" (Luke 24:17). For other examples of these types of conversation-starter questions, see John 1:38 or John 21:5.

2. Jesus used questions to introduce a topic. Occasionally, Jesus used a question to introduce an issue he wanted to talk about. Typically these questions were rhetorical (that is, Jesus didn't expect them to be answered) and seemed to act as attention-getters with his audience. For example, in Mark 4:30, Jesus introduces his parables by asking, "What shall we say the kingdom of God is like, or what parable shall we use to describe it?" He asks similar questions in Luke 13:18, 20. Today, teachers and speakers often use questions like these in the same way, introducing a topic by phrasing it in the form of a question, such as "How can you make marriage last?" or "How can we know God's will?" Even advertisers use this technique to grab people's attention. Who hasn't seen commercials that start out with questions like "Tired of musty shoe odor?" or "Looking for a new car?" These questions grab people's attention and focus their thoughts on whatever topic the question addresses.

> *"It seems that Jesus' questions all go back to where we started—with his purpose for teaching. All his questions match that purpose, because they caused people to look inward and think, with the result that their thinking and soul-searching would draw them closer to God. And that, to me, looks like a pretty good design for how we use questions and how we should teach: 'Will this question draw students closer to God?' "*
>
> —Thom Schultz

3. Jesus used questions to get specific information. Sometimes Jesus used fact-finding questions as a part of his teaching. For example, he asked the disciples how many loaves they had before feeding the four thousand. And he asked the demon-possessed man his name. Surprisingly, though, he didn't use these types of questions very often. Depending on which theologian you talk to, the Gospels record a total of anywhere from one hundred to over three hundred questions that Jesus asked.[6] But out of all those questions, there are only a few times that Jesus asked questions to elicit facts or information. Here are some examples:

Fact-Finding Questions	Reference
How many loaves do you have?	Matthew 15:34
What is your name?	Mark 5:9
Who touched my clothes?	Mark 5:30
What are you arguing with them about?	Mark 9:16

When I sent you without purse, bag or sandals, did you   Luke 22:35
lack anything?

Woman, where are they? Has no one condemned you?   John 8:10

Jesus' limited use of fact-finding questions in his teaching presents a remarkable contrast to what happens in the typical modern classroom. Most of today's students are regularly barraged with questions that focus entirely on factual recall. In fact, that's been the status quo in education for years. We can all remember what it was like: sitting in the classroom, hearing the teacher pose fact-finding question after fact-finding question, and usually trying to look very small so that we wouldn't be called on when we didn't know the answer. Unfortunately, that kind of educational upbringing has led most of us to believe that successful learning depends primarily on a student's ability to remember details about events, procedures, or what someone has said.

But while factual recall can be an important aspect of learning, it is not what the heart of education is all about. At least, not according to Jesus. As Zuck writes:

> Seldom did Jesus ask recall questions, merely asking for a recital of facts. If he did ask a "What-do-you-remember?" question, it was to lead on to interaction on an important issue. More often he challenged his students with "What-do-you-think?" questions. The disciples never had to guess at an answer, trying to discover what he had in mind. Instead, they were encouraged to think for themselves, to offer their own opinions and ideas.[7]

The questions Jesus asked rarely focused on recalling facts—instead, his questions focused on helping students analyze, understand, and apply truth to their lives.

Some people might say that Jesus didn't ask many fact-oriented questions because he was omniscient and therefore didn't need to ask such things. But whether Jesus had pre-knowledge of people's answers is irrelevant. After all, modern teachers also have "pre-knowledge" of the answers when they ask fact-based questions. So why didn't Jesus quiz students on facts, as most modern teachers do? Because, in most cases, *those types of questions don't really help people learn.*

Jesus only used teaching techniques that worked. He didn't waste his time using methods—or asking questions—that ultimately wouldn't help people discover truth and apply it to their lives. Although Jesus did ask fact-oriented questions on occasion, in most situations he knew that such questions would do little to inspire genuine learning. And even when he did ask fact-finding questions, they were almost always followed by a different sort of question or statement—one that provoked students to think and analyze information, rather than just recall facts.

Teacher's Corner: Should We Use Fact-Finding Questions When Teaching Children?

Even though Jesus didn't use fact-oriented questions too often in his teaching, that doesn't mean that fact-oriented questions aren't important—especially when it comes to teaching children.

I asked Christine Yount, editor of Children's Ministry Magazine, to offer her thoughts on the subject. Here's what she said:

Should teachers use "fact-oriented" questions with children?

Yes, teachers should use "fact-oriented" questions with children. Asking fact-oriented questions, such as "what, who, where, or how many" helps teachers ascertain whether kids are listening and whether they're getting the basic facts of the story.

Why should we use these questions if Jesus didn't?

The majority of Jesus' teaching was to an adult audience. We must remember that, rather than taking Jesus' adult-oriented teaching methods and applying them directly to children. While Jesus is the best example for teaching people at any age, applying his principles to children requires some tweaking.

Understanding children's cognitive development helps teachers know how to teach children effectively. Our faith is full of abstract concepts. If we do not ask the "checking" questions to ensure that children are "getting it," then we make dangerous assumptions and cannot ensure the outcomes in faith development that we hope to achieve.

There are critical and trivial facts that children need to know in each Bible story. For example, is it critical that children understand that in the story of Noah's ark that it rained for forty days and forty nights? Probably not. Is it critical that they understand that God was destroying the Earth because of wickedness but preserving Noah's family because of righteousness. Yes, definitely. Is it critical that they understand that Noah obeyed God? Yes. Is it critical to understand that the ark was made from gopher wood? You answer that.

If we do not ask the fact-finding questions, we may never know what kids are building their faith on.

Should teachers use only fact-oriented questions?

The answer is obvious. Fact-oriented questions need to be just a couple of quick questions to make sure kids are tracking with the essentials of the story. From there, teachers need to go on to the understanding questions. The best questions a teacher could ask children would have an element of fact-finding and a large measure of understanding.

Remember the parable of the Good Samaritan? After Jesus told that parable, he didn't ask, "Which people left the poor man on the road?" or even "What was the good Samaritan riding?" (That's a "who cares?" question.) Jesus masterfully asked, "Which of these three do you think proved to be a neighbor to the man who fell into the robbers' hands?" This question is a beautiful example for teachers of children. In one fell swoop, Jesus ascertains whether his student was listening and whether he understood the point. We should ask more questions of children like Jesus' question.

4. Jesus used questions to inspire people to think. Plutarch wrote, "The mind is a fire to be kindled, not a vessel to be filled."[8] Jesus frequently crafted questions that "kindled" the fires of learning by provoking his listeners to think. He was a master at asking questions that jolted people out of their comfort zones and caused them to look at their lives in new ways. Just imagine how his listeners were impacted when Jesus asked questions like these:

• "Why do you look at the speck of sawdust in your brother's eye and pay no attention to the plank in your own eye?" (Matthew 7:3)

• "What good will it be for a man if he gains the whole world, yet forfeits his soul?" (Matthew 16:26a)

• "Who of you by worrying can add a single hour to his life?" (Luke 12:25)

It's hard to examine those questions without feeling a bit uneasy. That's because questions like these have a way of compelling us to think critically about our lives and our behavior—even when such thoughts make us uncomfortable. And that's the whole reason Jesus used them. As Thom and Joani Schultz have noted: "Jesus didn't come to settle minds, but to jolt them. He didn't come to make us more comfortable, but to stir our thoughts, to help us learn, to make us think."[9]

Jesus used "thinking" questions to inspire people to see their common practices and beliefs from God's perspective. Rather than simply make declarative statements about truth, Jesus posed questions that held within them startling answers—answers that often propelled his listeners to consider truth in new ways.

5. Jesus used questions to challenge wrong thinking. Jesus also used "thinking" questions to challenge people's wrong beliefs or behavior. This was especially true in Jesus' frequent confrontations with the Pharisees and other religious leaders who opposed him. For example, consider this confrontation between Jesus and the chief priests in Matthew 21:23-27.

"Jesus entered the temple courts, and, while he was teaching, the chief priests and the elders of the people came to him. 'By what authority are you doing these things?' they asked. 'And who gave you this authority?' Jesus replied, 'I will also ask you one question. If you answer me, I will tell you by what authority I am doing these things. John's baptism—where did it come from? Was it from heaven, or from men?' They discussed it among themselves and said, 'If we say, "From heaven," he will ask, "Then why didn't you believe him?" But if we say, "From men"—we are afraid of the people, for they all hold that John was a prophet.' So they answered Jesus, 'We don't know.' Then he said, 'Neither will I tell you by what authority I am doing these things.' "

Notice that Jesus never answered their original question. Why? Because he recognized that their question sprang out of a wrong belief. So rather than deal with their question directly (which would have been fruitless), Jesus addressed the wrong belief behind the question—by asking a question of his own.

A similar scenario today might happen if a student asked, "Why doesn't God provide me a Mercedes?" or "Why doesn't God lead me to a better paying job?" Questions like these often stem from misguided beliefs

"I was really stunned to see how many times Jesus used questions and how confrontational he was... 'What's the matter with you?' 'Why don't you have more faith?' 'Why don't you understand yet?' And with the Pharisees, he just threw back in their faces the thing they had tried to catch him with. Again and again, he was confrontational with his questions."

—Paul Woods

about God's purpose and will for our lives. So instead of trying to answer the question directly, it could be far more effective to respond with a question that hits at the hidden issue: "Why did God send Jesus to save you—so you could be rich or so you could serve others in humility?" Jesus confronted wrong thinking with questions like these—that challenged people to rethink their wrong beliefs or assumptions about life.

6. Jesus used questions to expose people's sin. Sometimes Jesus used questions as a form of rebuke against the sin in people's lives. Again, this was especially true of Jesus' encounters with the Pharisees and other religious leaders. When Jesus would discern sinful motives or behaviors in people, he would sometimes expose their sin by posing a question. Here are a few examples:

- "Why do you entertain evil thoughts in your hearts?" (Matthew 9:4b)
- "You brood of vipers, how can you who are evil say anything good?" (Matthew 12:34a)
- "And why do you break the command of God for the sake of your tradition?" (Matthew 15:3)
- "You hypocrites, why are you trying to trap me?" (Matthew 22:18b)
- "Judas, are you betraying the Son of Man with a kiss?" (Luke 22:48)
- "Why are you trying to kill me?" (John 7:19b)

In asking these questions, Jesus wasn't necessarily looking for an answer; after all, he already knew what was in their hearts. Rather, the questions were intended to expose the wrong motives or behaviors he saw in others and (hopefully) provoke them to examine their own actions.

7. Jesus used questions to test people's understanding. In John 6, Jesus asks his disciples an interesting question. A massive crowd of more than five thousand people had gathered around Jesus to hear his teaching. It had probably been a long time since the crowd had been able to eat, and so Jesus asked Philip, "Where shall we buy bread for these people to eat?" (John 6:5). Philip answered, "Eight months' wages would not buy enough bread for each one to have a bite!"

Why would Jesus ask such a question? No doubt he knew it would be ridiculous to think that the disciples could afford to buy food for so many. Philip's response only echoes that fact. But Jesus asked the question not to find out about the availability of bread, but to test Philip's (and the disciples') understanding about who Jesus was. Jesus wanted to see whether Philip and the disciples would respond to the people's need with faith or with human reasoning. John 6:6 reveals Jesus' intent plainly: "He [Jesus] asked this only to test him, for he already had in mind what he was going to do."

Using questions can be a great way to "test" students' understanding of a principle or biblical truth. Here are some other examples where Jesus used "testing" questions:

• "Who do people say the Son of Man is?...But what about you? Who do you say I am?" (Matthew 16:13, 15)

• "What do you think about the Christ? Whose son is he?" (Matthew 22:42a)

In modern classrooms, these types of questions are often used in connection with case studies or discussions of real-life events—for example, "What should we do to abolish hunger in the world?" or "How should we treat doctors who perform abortions?" Such questions provide a great way to test students' understanding of the principles you teach so that both you and they will know whether true learning is taking place.

8. Jesus used questions to encourage faith. Many times Jesus' questions acted as gentle or forceful rebukes targeted at his disciples' lack of faith in God. When Peter began to sink into the waves in Matthew 14:30-31, Jesus reached out and caught him, and then asked, "Why did you doubt?" And in John 11:39-40, when Martha cautioned Jesus against opening Lazarus' tomb, Jesus chided her by asking, "Did I not tell you that if you believed, you would see the glory of God?"

Today's teachers could use questions like these in the same way Jesus did. For example, when a student is worried about finding a job or passing a test in school, we could encourage that person to believe in God by asking, "Why worry? Do you believe that God will take care of you?" or "God has provided for you this far—why would he stop now?"

Jesus-Style Questions[10]

Recently at a National Youth and Children's Ministry Convention, a group of educators gathered to study Jesus' questions and see if they could learn how to craft

"Jesus-style" questions in their own teaching more effectively. As part of their studies, they each wrote one question that they thought Jesus might ask if he were teaching their class. Here's a sampling of the questions they came up with. See whether you think their questions fit into one of the categories of "Jesus-style" questions we've discussed.

What does it mean to be alive?

Why are you here today?

What is it about Jesus' love for you that makes you ashamed to share it?

When was the last time you felt the Holy Spirit?

Why don't you witness for me?

What is your direction?

Why do you think you know Jesus?

Why do we love?

How have you served me today?

Is love an act or an emotion?

What can you count on?

Why is it hard for you to do the things God asks of you?

Why are you here? What do you expect to learn?

Who is your neighbor?

Why do you criticize your own people?

Do you love me?

What makes you believe in me?

What makes you doubt God's love for you?

How do you demonstrate your love for me?

What happened to your belief in me?

Why do you come to church?

Translating Jesus' Questioning Skills Into the Modern Classroom

Now that we know more about the types of questions Jesus asked, how can we translate his techniques into our classrooms? It's really easier than you might think. Although Jesus crafted his questions specifically for each person and situation he faced, we can draw out several practical principles from his teaching that we can apply right away. Here they are.

1. Ask purposeful questions. If you were allowed only one question to ask your students, what would it be? As Christian teachers following our Master, we should view questions as he did—as effective tools for

learning that should be used wisely and purposefully. As one Christian teacher has commented, we should not ask "just any questions. They must be the right kind of questions." That means that for every lesson we prepare, we need to think through not only what we want to ask, but how we want to ask it. Questions are like arrows that pierce the thinking and the heart. Even if the arrow is straight, it will still miss the target if the bow is poorly strung.

How can you make your questions purposeful? By starting with the end in mind. Ask yourself, "What principle or truth do I want my students to grasp?" Then consider what kinds of questions might lead students toward learning that principle. For example, if you want students to grasp the truth that we all need God's forgiveness to have true life, then you might ask questions like these:

• If you had to choose between being forgiven and being healthy, which would you choose? Explain.

• How does the lack of forgiveness destroy life?

• What would the world be like if God never forgave?

• What would your life be like if God never forgave you?

Purposeful questions aren't really about debating whether a biblical truth is right or wrong. Instead, they aim at provoking students to consider how a truth or principle should be worked out in their lives. There is a "point" to such questions that goes far beyond simply finding the "right" answer or promoting empty discussion.

2. Ask questions that make people think. We've noted that Jesus only occasionally used "one-right-answer" questions in his teaching. Far more often, Jesus posed questions that inspired thinking. We can do the same in our teaching by following a few simple strategies:

• Ask open-ended questions—These are questions that require more than a "yes," "no," or a factual recall. "Where did Jesus die?" is a closed-ended question. It requires little thinking to come up with the answer. An open-ended question on the same topic might be, "Why did Jesus have to suffer on a cross? Why couldn't he have died peacefully in his sleep? Wouldn't that still be 'dying for the sins of the world'? Why or why not?"

Open-ended questions require listeners to think because there isn't one "right" answer, but rather an assortment of possibilities, that, when considered, can lead students to a greater understanding of the truth.

• Don't evaluate students' responses directly—to ask "thinking" questions successfully, you must allow people time to think and process what you've asked. If a student responds rashly (as Philip did when Jesus asked him where they could buy enough bread to feed the crowd of five thousand), don't pass judgment on the response. Instead, let the person continue to think through his or her own answer, reconsider it, and, hopefully, come to a better answer in time. You might even ask additional questions to help the student rethink his or her answer.

This guideline is difficult for teachers to follow. Because we really want our students to learn, many times we feel compelled to reveal the answer or explain the principle we're asking about—especially if we fear students aren't "getting it." But sometimes when we "give away the answer," we effectively shut down the learning process in our students' minds. It's like being told the solution to a riddle before you've had the chance to think it through yourself. To keep the learning process going, avoid labeling your students' responses as "good" or "bad." Instead, respond with a neutral "uh-huh" or "thank you," and allow students to keep processing their own responses so that genuine learning can take place.

But what if someone offers a response that's truly unbiblical or misguided? Rather than passing judgment on a student's answer, ask follow-up questions to help the student think more critically about what he or she is saying. Or ask the rest of the class to comment on the student's answer. Either way, you've avoided shutting down thinking, while still helping to guide your students toward understanding the truth.

3. Ask questions that challenge. If a question doesn't challenge you, it probably won't challenge your class either. This is true whether you're teaching adults, youth, or even children. (After all, some of the best lessons about life can be found in children's books!) Jesus' questions were designed to propel people toward thinking in new ways, or to present them with new ideas or truths that they'd probably never considered before. Our questions should be carefully crafted to do the same thing. Good questions should "raise the bar" of Christian commitment, faith, and understanding. They're not designed just to help people find a "better" answer; they're designed to help God make better people.

However, here's one note of caution: Just because a question is challenging doesn't mean it has to be complicated. In fact, the best questions are usually quite simple:

- "Why did you doubt?" (Matthew 14:31b)
- "If I am telling the truth, why don't you believe me?" (John 8:46b)
- "You of little faith, why are you so afraid?" (Matthew 8:26a)

Jesus asked simple, direct questions that challenged people and promoted genuine learning. As teachers who want to follow in his steps, so can we.

4. Don't always ask questions that require immediate answers. According to one theologian's research, of 225 different questions Jesus asked in his teaching, less than half were ever answered![11] Jesus was a master at asking thought-provoking questions that he never intended to be answered right away. Instead, these questions were designed to inspire thinking, confront sin, point out truth, or encourage faith in people's lives. As modern teachers, we have a hard time thinking of using questions for any purpose other than to get answers. But more often than not, Jesus used questions that weren't designed to elicit an immediate response, but rather provoke the listener to consider the truth contained in the question itself. For example:

- "Is not life more important than food, and the body more important than clothes?" (Matthew 6:25b)
- "What good will it be for a man if he gains the whole world, yet forfeits his soul?" (Matthew 16:26a)

To teach as Jesus taught, we can also learn to use "truth-packed" questions like these to push students toward genuine learning. For example, here are some questions that might apply to your students' lives:

- Children: "Aren't your friends more important than your toys?"
- Youth: "What good is looking for a wife (or husband) if you can't hold out for the right person?"
- Adult: "What good is a promise if you don't have to keep it?"

"If the great goal for a question is to draw people closer to God, there are plenty of questions that don't have to have any particular answer or the 'right' answer. If the question triggers the process that eventually draws someone closer to God, then the question has accomplished its purpose."

—Thom Schultz

Questions like these don't necessarily require an immediate answer, but they provoke students to ponder their meaning and learn valuable lessons over time.

5. Use different kinds of questions frequently. As we've already noted, Jesus used a variety of questions for a variety of purposes. We can easily follow in his steps simply by making sure our teaching also includes a variety of questions. One rule of thumb might be to try to include each of the following types of questions in every lesson we teach:

- Conversation-starter—"In what ways did you interact with your parents this week?"
- Topic-launcher—"How can we honor our parents?"
- Fact-finder—"What does God's Word say about honoring parents?"
- Thought-provoker—"What makes you feel 'honored' by others?" "How can you apply that to 'honoring' your parents?"
- Sin-confronter—"How can you claim to love your parents if you will not honor them in daily life?"
- Faith-encourager—"Don't you believe that God will bless you for honoring your parents?"

6. Encourage questions from others. Too often, we teachers are so concerned about "getting through the lesson" that we inadvertently discourage students from asking questions. As a result, valuable learning opportunities are squelched. However, Jesus welcomed questions from others and often used them as a launching point for learning. (For a few examples of this, see Matthew 13:10-17 or John 3:1-21.) We can do the same by creating in our classrooms an atmosphere of openness in which questions are welcome and valued. To teach like Jesus, shift your focus from "getting through the lesson" to "getting through to students." By making that simple shift in attitude, we can begin to welcome students' questions more easily and use them as powerful opportunities for learning.

Jesus' example clearly teaches us that asking the right questions in the right ways is critical to effective teaching. The value of crafting good questions was expressed well by DeGarmo when he wrote: "To question well is to teach well."[12] That statement really sums up what this chapter emphasizes about teaching the way Jesus taught. And so we'll list it as Principle 7:

Principle 7
To teach well, question well.

In the next chapter, we'll explore what some consider to be the most elusive aspect of Jesus' teaching style—how he modeled what he taught. Through that exploration, we'll gain some life-changing insights into the significant but often-overlooked impact we can have on students by purposefully modeling the truths and principles we want them to learn.

The Questions Jesus Asked

Although this list is not exhaustive, it includes most of the questions Jesus asked during the years of his teaching ministry. Study these questions and the surrounding verses to see how Jesus used questions in his teaching, then consider how you might adapt Jesus' questioning style to your own classroom. You might even consider using some of Jesus' questions just as they are!

Question	Reference
If the salt loses its saltiness, how can it be made salty again?	Matthew 5:13; Mark 9:50; Luke 14:34
If you love those who love you, what reward will you get? Are not even the tax collectors doing that? And if you greet only your brothers, what are you doing more than others? Do not even pagans do that?	Matthew 5:46-47; Luke 6:32
Is not life more important than food, and the body more important than clothes?	Matthew 6:25
Are you not much more valuable than they?	Matthew 6:26
Who of you by worrying can add a single hour to his life?	Matthew 6:27
If that is how God clothes the grass of the field...will he not much more clothe you, O you of little faith?	Matthew 6:30
Why do you look at the speck of sawdust in your brother's eye and pay no attention to the plank in your own eye? How can you say to your brother, "Let me take the speck out of your eye," when all the time there is a plank in your own eye?	Matthew 7:3-4; Luke 6:41-42
Which of you, if his son asks for bread, will give him a stone? Or if he asks for a fish, will give him a snake?	Matthew 7:9-10; Luke 11:11

Do people pick grapes from thornbushes, or figs from thistles?	Matthew 7:16
You of little faith, why are you so afraid?	Matthew 8:26; Mark 4:40
Why do you entertain evil thoughts in your hearts?	Matthew 9:4; Mark 2:8; Luke 5:22
Which is easier: to say, "Your sins are forgiven," or to say, "Get up and walk"?	Matthew 9:5; Mark 2:9; Luke 5:23
How can the guests of the bridegroom mourn while he is with them?	Matthew 9:15; Mark 2:19; Luke 5:34
Do you believe that I am able to do this?	Matthew 9:28
Are not two sparrows sold for a penny?	Matthew 10:29
What did you go out into the desert to see? A reed swayed by the wind? If not, what did you go out to see? A man dressed in fine clothes? No, those who wear fine clothes are in king's palaces. Then what did you go out to see? A prophet?	Matthew 11:7-9; Luke 7:24-26
To what can I compare this generation?	Matthew 11:16; Luke 7:31
Haven't you read what David did when he and his companions were hungry?	Matthew 12:3; Mark 2:25; Luke 6:3
If Satan drives out Satan, he is divided against himself. How then can his kingdom stand? And if I drive out demons by Beelzebub, by whom do your people drive them out?	Matthew 12:26-27; Luke 11:18-19
Or again, how can anyone enter a strong man's house and carry off his possessions unless he first ties up the strong man?	Matthew 12:29
You brood of vipers, how can you who are evil say anything good?	Matthew 12:34
Who is my mother, and who are my brothers?	Matthew 12:48; Mark 3:33
Have you understood all these things?	Matthew 13:51
Why did you doubt?	Matthew 14:31
And why do you break the command of God for the sake of your tradition?	Matthew 15:3
Are you still so dull? Don't you see that whatever enters the mouth goes into the stomach and then out of the body?	Matthew 15:16-17; Mark 7:18
How many loaves do you have?	Matthew 15:34; Mark 8:5
You of little faith, why are you talking among yourselves about having no bread?	Matthew 16:8; Mark 8:17
Do you still not understand?	Matthew 16:9; Mark 8:17

Who do people say the Son of Man is?	Matthew 16:13; Mark 8:27; Luke 9:18
But what about you? Who do you say I am?	Matthew 16:15; Mark 8:29; Luke 9:20
What good will it be for a man if he gains the whole world, yet forfeits his soul?	Matthew 16:26; Mark 8:36; Luke 9:25
Or what can a man give in exchange for his soul?	Matthew 16:26; Mark 8:37
O unbelieving and perverse generation...how long shall I stay with you?	Matthew 17:17; Mark 9:19; Luke 9:41
What do you think?	Matthew 18:12
Why do you ask me about what is good?	Matthew 19:17; Mark 10:18; Luke 18:19
What is it you want?	Matthew 20:21; Mark 10:36
Can you drink the cup I am going to drink?	Matthew 20:22; Mark 10:38
What do you want me to do for you?	Matthew 20:32; Mark 10:51; Luke 18:41
John's baptism—where did it come from? Was it from heaven, or from men?	Matthew 21:25; Mark 11:30; Luke 20:4
You hypocrites, why are you trying to trap me?	Matthew 22:18; Mark 12:15
Whose portrait is this? And whose inscription?	Matthew 22:20; Mark 12:16; Luke 20:24
What do you think about the Christ? Whose son is he?	Matthew 22:42
You blind fools! Which is greater: the gold, or the temple that makes the gold sacred?	Matthew 23:17
You snakes! You brood of vipers! How will you escape being condemned to hell?	Matthew 23:33
Do you see all these things?	Matthew 24:2; Mark 13:2
Why are you bothering this woman?	Matthew 26:10; Mark 14:6
Could you men not keep watch with me for one hour?	Matthew 26:40; Mark 14:37
Which is lawful on the Sabbath: to do good or to do evil, to save life or to kill?	Mark 3:4; Luke 6:9
How can Satan drive out Satan?	Mark 3:23
Do you still have no faith?	Mark 4:40; Luke 8:25
What is your name?	Mark 5:9; Luke 8:30
Who touched my clothes?	Mark 5:30; Luke 8:45
Why does this generation ask for a miraculous	Mark 8:12

sign?

Are your hearts hardened? Do you have eyes but fail to see, and ears but fail to hear?	Mark 8:17-18
What are you arguing with them about?	Mark 9:16
What were you arguing about on the road?	Mark 9:33
What did Moses command you?	Mark 10:3
If you do good to those who are good to you, what credit is that to you?	Luke 6:33
And if you lend to those from whom you expect repayment, what credit is that to you?	Luke 6:34
Why do you call me, "Lord, Lord," and do not what I say?	Luke 6:46
Do you see this woman?	Luke 7:44
What is written in the Law? How do you read it?	Luke 10:26
Did not the one who made the outside make the inside also?	Luke 11:40
Who of you by worrying can add a single hour to his life? Since you cannot do this very little thing, why do you worry about the rest?	Luke 12:25-26
How is it that you don't know how to interpret this present time?	Luke 12:56
Why don't you judge for yourselves what is right?	Luke 12:57
Were not all ten cleansed? Where are the other nine? Was no one found to return and give praise to God except this foreigner?	Luke 17:17-18
And will not God bring about justice for his chosen ones, who cry out to him day and night? Will he keep putting them off?	Luke 18:7
However, when the Son of Man comes, will he find faith on the earth?	Luke 18:8
When I sent you without purse, bag or sandals, did you lack anything?	Luke 22:35
Judas, are you betraying the Son of Man with a kiss?	Luke 22:48
For if men do these things when the tree is green, what will happen when it is dry?	Luke 23:31
What are you discussing together as you walk along?	Luke 24:17
Why are you troubled, and why do doubts rise in	Luke 24:38

your minds?

You are Israel's teacher...and do you not understand these things?	John 3:10
I have spoken to you of earthly things and you do not believe; how then will you believe if I speak of heavenly things?	John 3:12
Will you give me a drink?	John 4:7
Do you want to get well?	John 5:6
How can you believe if you accept praise from one another, yet make no effort to obtain the praise that comes from the only God?	John 5:44
Where shall we buy bread for these people to eat?	John 6:5
Does this offend you?	John 6:61
Why are you trying to kill me?	John 7:19
Woman, where are they? Has no one condemned you?	John 8:10
If I am telling the truth, why don't you believe me?	John 8:46
Do you believe in the Son of Man?	John 9:35
For which of these [miracles] do you stone me?	John 10:32
Do you believe this?	John 11:26
Did I not tell you that if you believed, you would see the glory of God?	John 11:40
Do you understand what I have done for you?	John 13:12
Will you really lay down your life for me?	John 13:38
Don't you know me, Philip, even after I have been among you such a long time?	John 14:9
Shall I not drink the cup the Father has given me?	John 18:11
But if I spoke the truth, why did you strike me?	John 18:23
Is that your own idea, or did others talk to you about me?	John 18:34
Woman...why are you crying? Who is it you are looking for?	John 20:15
Friends, haven't you any fish?	John 21:5
Simon son of John, do you truly love me more than these?	John 21:15
If I want him to remain alive until I return, what is that to you?	John 21:22

[1] Norman Sorenson, "How Christ Used Questions" (Th.M. thesis, Dallas Theological Seminary, TX, 1953) 45. Quoted in *Teaching as Jesus Taught,* 237.

[2] Charles DeGarmo, *Interest and Education* (New York, NY: Macmillan, 1911), 179. Quoted in *Teaching as Jesus Taught,* 235.

[3] Roy B. Zuck, *Teaching as Jesus Taught* (Grand Rapids, MI: Baker Books, 1995), 236.

[4] Meredith D. Gall, "The Use of Questions in Teaching," *Review of Educational Research* 40 (December 1970), 72. Quoted in *Teaching as Jesus Taught,* 235-236.

[5] D. Perkins, *Smart Schools* (New York, NY: The Free Press, 1992), 32. Quoted in *Why Nobody Learns Much of Anything at Church: And How to Fix It,* 92.

[6] The differences in opinion about the number of questions Jesus asked is mostly due to variations in translation of Jesus' words from the Greek text, and whether the Bible scholars chose to weed out redundant examples of the same question recorded in multiple Gospels.

[7] Zuck, *Teaching as Jesus Taught,* 255.

[8] *Illustrations Unlimited,* ed. by James S. Hewett (Wheaton, IL: Tyndale House Publishers, 1988), 315. Used by permission. All rights reserved.

[9] Schultz, *Why Nobody Learns Much of Anything at Church: And How to Fix It,* 91.

[10] Information taken from a workshop led by Rick Lawrence and the author in January, 1997.

[11] Zuck, *Teaching as Jesus Taught,* 258-276.

[12] DeGarmo, *Interest and Education,* 179. Quoted in *Teaching as Jesus Taught,* 256.

Chapter 8
Showing the Way

"Philip said, 'Lord, show us the Father
and that will be enough for us.' Jesus answered:
'Don't you know me, Philip, even after I have been
among you such a long time? Anyone who has seen me
has seen the Father. How can you say, "Show us the Father"?
Don't you believe that I am in the Father,
and that the Father is in me? The words I say to you
are not just my own. Rather, it is the Father, living in me,
who is doing his work.' "
—*John 14:8-10*

I once heard a true story about a missionary who got lost in the African jungle while trying to reach a remote village. After wandering around in the bush for some time, he caught sight of a hut, and quickly went to ask if there was anyone who could lead him out of the jungle to his destination. The father of the family, who was native to the area, agreed to help.

"Thank you," said the missionary. "Please show me the way."

"Walk," said the native, and abruptly started off into the bush. For more than an hour, the missionary followed the man, hacking his way through the thick growth of unmarked jungle. Eventually the missionary began to worry that the native didn't really know where he was going.

"Are you sure this is the way?" asked the missionary.

"Yes," said the native.

"But where is the path?" he asked.

The native stopped and said, "Bwana, in this place there is no path. I am the path."[1]

In John 14:6, Jesus said, "I am the way and the truth and the life. No one comes to the Father except through me." At times in our lives as Christians, we may find it hard to understand exactly what Jesus meant by this statement. How can a person also be a "path" or way for us to follow? But the story of the native and the missionary provides a picture that may shed light on Jesus' words…

In this world, there is no path. Jesus is the path.

Jesus' teaching went beyond the parables he told, the commands he gave, or the discourses he delivered. He was not merely a philosopher like Aristotle who expounded on ideas about the meaning of life. Nor was he simply a self-proclaimed prophet like Mohammed who told secrets about life that he learned while fasting in a cave. Jesus *was* life. *He* was the message. He taught people what true life *in him* looked like through the way he lived—through every choice, every action, every gesture or laugh. He modeled eternal life for us so that we could know what it looks like, learn how to recognize it, and discover how to enter into it for ourselves.

In Luke 9:23-24 Jesus said,

"If anyone would come after me, he must deny himself and take up his cross daily and follow me. For whoever wants to save his life will lose it, but whoever loses his life for me will save it."

To be a disciple of Christ means more than following Jesus' teachings. It means following a person. It means realizing on the deepest level of our souls that Jesus didn't come just to show us the way; he came to be the way for us. He didn't come just to teach a message; he is the message he came to share.

As teachers who are committed to following in his steps, we, too, must realize that our lives project a message to those we teach. And whatever we hope our students will learn from us, we can be assured that the one lesson they will remember above all others is the one we teach by the way we live.

Think back to a teacher who had an impact on your own life. What do you remember about him or her? Was it a lesson he taught? Was it some project she assigned? Probably not. Then what do you remember? Perhaps you recall what the person was like, how she connected with you personally, or how he showed compassion or helped you out when he didn't have to.

I had one biology teacher in high school who I will always remember. Her name was Ms. Rohrer (pronounced "roar"), and in the front of her classroom she had a huge placard that read, "Boy, am I enthusiastic!"—in big, colorful letters, so it couldn't be missed. Every time students entered her class, she would lead us all in a cheer: "Boy, are we enthusiastic!" She'd wave her arms and smile, and we'd all yell it together. And if we didn't yell it loud enough, we'd do it again and again until we did. It was a ritual that made Ms. Rohrer an annoyance to other teachers nearby. But it made her a favorite among the kids.

Even though Ms. Rohrer was a superb teacher, I can't recall too many facts about biology from that class. But I can tell you all about a wonderful Christian woman who taught me about joy—because "joy" is what she was.

As Christian teachers, there are a few critical questions we must each ask ourselves:

- What lesson are you teaching with your life?
- Is it the lesson Jesus wants you to teach?
- What needs to happen in your life to make you a more effective "model" for Jesus?

To answer these questions, we'll explore how Jesus modeled life for his disciples, and draw out the lessons or principles he wanted his disciples (and us) to learn by the way he lived. Then we'll translate those principles to our own lives as teachers to discover several practical ways we can follow in his steps.

> *"Jesus was the Word of God in human form. He was 'It.' He lived the Word; he modeled it. And I wonder how we as teachers see ourselves now. Do we also strive to be as close as we can to that model of God?"*
> —Joani Schultz

But Wait a Minute! I'm Not Perfect!

Modeling—or teaching through example—can be the most frightening aspect of teaching, because it requires a level of vulnerability and openness to scrutiny that most of us would rather avoid. After all, none of us is perfect, and there's no changing that no matter how many times well-meaning folks might point it out to us.

Of course, Jesus didn't have weaknesses or secret sins that he wanted to hide. His example of God was flawless. As the writer of Hebrews puts it, "The Son is the radiance of God's glory and the exact representation of his being" (Hebrews 1:3). As a result, Jesus didn't wrestle with fear over criticism or the scrutiny of others the way we might. He lived a perfect life. He revealed the Father flawlessly. And he welcomed his followers to examine his life, so that they could discover God's Truth for themselves. As William Barclay writes,

> Jesus did not tell his disciples who he was; he encouraged, and even compelled, them to discover it for themselves. True knowledge of Jesus comes not from a text-book, and not even from another person, but from personal confrontation with him.[2]

For Jesus, these "personal confrontations" held no fear of embarrassment or humiliation. After all, he was perfect. For Christ, modeling God was as natural as breathing.

For us, it is not quite so. Despite our best attempts to hide it, deep down we all know that we are each fraught with weaknesses, failures, and the inability to measure up no matter how hard we try. We are not like Jesus in this way. We are not perfect. And any example we set for others will be, at best, imprecise, and at worst, seriously damaging.

That's why the idea of teaching through modeling can be so terrifying to so many of us. What if students see my fears, my self-doubt? What if they judge me or publicly criticize my past? What if they reject my teaching because they don't agree with the way I live? Haunting questions like these might make us wonder whether we should try to model our teaching at all. But the Bible makes it clear that modeling the truth by the way we live should be an integral part of every Christian's life—especially for leaders in the church.

"Follow my example, as I follow the example of Christ" (1 Corinthians 11:1).

"Don't let anyone look down on you because you are young, but set an example for the believers in speech, in life, in love, in faith and in purity" (1 Timothy 4:12).

"In everything set them an example by doing what is good. In your teaching show integrity, seriousness and soundness of speech that cannot be condemned, so that those who oppose you may be ashamed because they have nothing bad to say about us" (Titus 2:7-8).

"Be shepherds of God's flock that is under your care, serving as over-seers—not because you must, but because you are willing, as God wants you to be; not greedy for money, but eager to serve; not lording it over those entrusted to you, but being examples to the flock" (1 Peter 5:2-3).

After washing the disciples' feet, Jesus also emphasized the importance of following in his steps before others. In John 13:15-16, he says:

"I have set you an example that you should do as I have done for you. I tell you the truth, no servant is greater than his master, nor is a messenger greater than the one who sent him."

Since "no servant is greater than his master," it seems clear that if Jesus taught through modeling, so should we. But what about our imperfections? How can we model God's truth the way Jesus did, when our lives are constantly plagued by sin and human weakness?

Perhaps the answer can be found in Paul's words in 2 Corinthians 4:7.

"But we have this treasure in jars of clay to show that this all-surpassing power is from God and not from us."

In that simple statement, Paul explains the reason why we should model what we teach, just like Jesus did, even though our example won't be perfect.

You see, God knew we wouldn't be able to match Jesus' perfection. As teachers following in his steps, we'll never be able to fully demonstrate with our lives the truths we teach from God's Word. But that's OK. In fact, that's the way God designed it. It's through our *weakness* that God's strength is revealed.

"Brothers, think of what you were when you were called. Not many of you were wise by human standards; not many were influential; not many were of noble birth. But God chose the foolish things of the world to shame the wise; God chose the weak things of the world to shame the strong. He chose the lowly things of this world and the despised things—and the things that are not—to nullify the things that are, so that no one may boast before him. Therefore, as it is written: 'Let him who boasts boast in the Lord' " (1 Corinthians 1:26-29, 31).

In our teaching then, the example we model is not supposed to show students how well we "have it all together" in Christ. Instead, our example is designed to show God's greatness and mercy in forgiving and saving people who are so utterly flawed and undeserving—people just like us.

Does that kind of modeling require vulnerability? Yes. Will it mean that people will see your weaknesses and failures? Without a doubt. But more than any weakness, modeling what you teach will allow people to see how Jesus can work powerfully through ordinary people—even though they're far from perfect.

"And they praised God because of me" (Galatians 1:24).

Jesus the Role Model

Warren Benson wrote, "Having time to walk the roads and sit at lunch daily with the King of kings has to be the most enviable privilege imaginable."[3] How true! Who of us wouldn't love to trade places with the disciples for just one day—to be able to walk with Jesus in the flesh, hear his voice, and watch his life. But if we were able to watch Jesus and observe him daily, as his disciples did, what would we discover about him? What would we learn about what it means to follow him?

To discover what Jesus taught through modeling is not as simple as examining his parables or pondering the questions he asked. That's because parables and questions have a beginning and an ending. We can separate them, explore them individually, and draw out the specific lessons each one contains. But for Jesus, teaching by example was a constant affair, without a discernible beginning or ending. Everything Jesus did—every gesture he made, every touch he gave, every emotion he expressed—modeled what he taught.

"He [Jesus] was always teaching. I mean, he grabbed teachable moments all the time. But who he was, what he did, how he interacted was always the lesson, whether it was through an experience of washing the disciples' feet or just watching him 'be'—he was teaching. And that's a reminder for all of us: It's not what you do in the classroom. It's who you are out there that will probably be the most powerful lesson."

—Joani Schultz

Nevertheless, we can discern several lessons Jesus taught his disciples through the way he lived, by looking closely at Jesus' choices in life and by watching the way his disciples responded to his example. Let's take a brief look at some of the lessons Jesus taught with his life and consider how we can follow his example in our own teaching.

1. Jesus modeled the importance of prayer and intimacy with God. Several of the Gospels refer to Jesus going off alone to pray. For example, Jesus spent a night in prayer before he chose the twelve apostles (Luke 6:12). His experience of walking on water occurred after a long prayer session (Matthew 14:23). One time he even chose to move his ministry to another part of the country after praying (Mark 1:35). In Luke 5:15-16, the apostle sums up Jesus' example by writing:

"The news about him spread all the more, so that crowds of people came to hear him and to be healed of their sicknesses. *But Jesus often withdrew to lonely places and prayed.*" (author emphasis)

The truth is we don't really know much about what happened during these prayer times. For example, we don't know specifically what Jesus prayed about, exactly how he expressed his prayers, or how God responded to him. What we do know is that staying close to God mattered a lot to Jesus, and prayer was the primary way he nurtured that intimacy.

As important as prayer and intimacy with God was to Jesus, he never initiated teaching his disciples about prayer. Instead, he modeled intimacy with God through the way he lived. And through his modeling, he whet their appetites to learn more.

"One day Jesus was praying in a certain place. When he finished, one of his disciples said to him, "Lord, teach us to pray, just as John taught his disciples" (Luke 11:1).

What followed was Jesus' famous teaching on the nature and importance of prayer. But that teaching would have had much less impact if Jesus hadn't first modeled intimacy with God in a way that captivated his disciples and inspired them to learn more.

Perhaps the most powerful way you can impact your students toward a genuine, personal relationship with God is by modeling deep and consistent prayer in your own life. Admittedly, that may not be as easy for you as it was for Jesus. After all, Jesus was around his disciples all the time, while you probably only get to be around your students a few hours each week. Still, there are some simple ways you can model intimacy with God for your students—and inspire them to deepen their own spiritual lives.

• Make your own prayer life a priority. Set aside regular time for "personal prayer retreats," just as Jesus did. Plan your retreats ahead of time, even if they only last an hour. Plan out where you will go and what you will pray about. Be sure to take along a Bible, pen, and paper so you can record your insights.

How often should you pray? Well, everyone's schedule is different, but I try to follow this simple guideline for scheduling my prayer time:

- one hour each day
- one day each month
- one week each year

That means that in addition to setting aside one hour for prayer each day, I set aside one full day for prayer each month and a one-week "personal retreat" each year. That schedule may sound impossible to some, but you'd be surprised what you can make time for if you make it a priority and plan ahead.

• Talk about your own prayer life. As you share stories from your life, speak of the times you spend in prayer. Help your students know that prayer is a normal and consistent part of your life.

• Pray often with students, especially when it's not part of the expected routine. Prayer is a vital part of any Christian group. Unfortunately, it can often fall into a ritual of habit as an opening or closing for a Bible study or lesson. Shake up the ritual by praying spontaneously during the lesson. If someone shares a need during class, stop right then and pray together for that person. Also, vary what you pray about and how you pray together. For example, instead of praying as a whole group, form pairs or trios and have students pray in huddles. And instead of praying for whatever comes to mind, try orchestrating the prayer time by calling out subjects for students to focus on, such as world leaders or spiritual renewal in America.

• Ask your students to pray for you. Before Jesus' arrest, he went off to pray and asked Peter, James, and John to "watch and pray" with him as he struggled with God (Matthew 26:36-41). In the same way, when you have a specific need or issue you're struggling over, ask your students to pray with you about it. That will help them to see value in their own prayer life and encourage them to pray for others more readily.

Teacher's Corner: Remember Your Goal

Remember your primary goal as a Christian teacher is "to draw people into a genuine, personal relationship with God" (Principle 2). Modeling can be a powerful tool to help you accomplish that goal in your teaching.

---

2. Jesus modeled the importance of devotion to God's will. After talking to the Samaritan woman, Jesus' disciples returned to find a crowd of people approaching him. The disciples no doubt knew that Jesus hadn't eaten in some time, and so they urged him to take a "time-out" to grab a bite to eat. But Jesus gave an interesting reply, which is recorded in John 4:32-35.

"But he said to them, 'I have food to eat that you know nothing about.' Then his disciples said to each other, 'Could someone have brought him food?' 'My food,' said Jesus, 'is to do the will of him who sent me and to finish his work. Do you not say, "Four months more and then the harvest"? I tell you, open your eyes and look at the fields! They are ripe for harvest.' "

Jesus' first concern was accomplishing God's will. Obeying God was so important to him that he called it his "food" or "nourishment." In another passage, after John the Baptist was beheaded, Jesus was sad and tried to get away from the crowds for a time. But they kept finding him and begging him to heal their sick. Even though he was stricken by grief and in need of prayer, notice his response, recorded in Matthew 14:13-14.

"When Jesus heard what had happened, he withdrew by boat privately to a solitary place. Hearing of this, the crowds followed him on foot from the towns. When Jesus landed and saw a large crowd, he had compassion on them and healed their sick."

Watching Christ's obedience to God's will, even in the midst of personal grief or exhaustion, may have inspired Peter to later write:

"Therefore, prepare your minds for action; be self-controlled; set your hope fully on the grace to be given you when Jesus Christ is revealed. As obedient children, do not conform to the evil desires you had when you lived in ignorance. But just as he who called you is holy, so be holy in all you do; for it is written: 'Be holy, because I am holy' " (1 Peter 1:13-16).

Modeling devotion to God's will takes dedication and a deep level of commitment in your own relationship with God. None of us has "arrived" to the point that we are completely devoted to God's will 100 percent of the time. We all struggle with sin and our own human limitations. But there are some things we can do as teachers to help our students see the importance of devotion to God's will.

• Pray for God's will in your class. When you pray with students, devote your class time to God, and ask him to reveal his will in your students' lives. Make seeking God's will a central part of your corporate prayer.

• Lead the group on a study of God's will. Instead of asking the question, "What is God's will for my life?" (as most people do), lead students to explore the answer to a different question: "What is God's will?" Then lead students on a study through Scripture to find the answer to that question.

• Talk about your own struggle to follow God's will, and confess when you fall short. Talking about your own efforts to seek and follow God's will can help your students feel more comfortable with their own struggles, and inspire them to make seeking God's will a central part of their lives.

• Lead the group in an organized fast. Fasting is an intense form of seeking God. It forces us to set aside our own agendas and focus our minds on God—his thoughts, his feelings, and his will. Elmer L. Towns writes, "One of the greatest spiritual benefits of fasting is becoming more attentive to God—becoming more aware of our own inadequacies and His adequacy, our own contingencies and His self-sufficiency—and listening to what He wants us to be and do."[4] There are many different types and lengths of fasts you can embark on with your class. Some may last for days, while others last only for a few hours. Choose a fast that you think will work best for your class members and try it. You can choose a focus for the fast, such as seeking God's will for your church or community. Or you can let group members focus on their individual needs before God. Either way, you'll inspire class members to understand and embrace the importance of seeking and following God's will in their lives.

3. Jesus modeled the importance of accepting sinners. In Luke

19:1-10, Luke tells the story of Jesus' encounter with Zacchaeus, the tax collector. In Jesus' day, few people liked tax collectors, because they were considered traitors who collaborated with the Roman empire to exploit the people. But when Jesus saw Zacchaeus, his response was rich with acceptance and genuine interest. "Zacchaeus," he said, "come down immediately. I must stay at your house today." And so the Scripture says that Zacchaeus came down and welcomed him gladly.

Jesus' response to Zacchaeus didn't do much for his own reputation, however. Luke 19:7 reports: "All the people saw this and began to mutter, 'He has gone to be the guest of a "sinner." ' " But Jesus didn't care. What mattered to him, in that moment, was extending acceptance toward a man who was deemed unacceptable. And, as a result, Zacchaeus put his faith in Christ.

In another similar scenario, Jesus went to have dinner with a Pharisee named Simon (Luke 7:37-38). As you read what happened, put yourself in Jesus' place. How would you have responded in this situation?

"When a woman who had lived a sinful life in that town learned that Jesus was eating at the Pharisee's house, she brought an alabaster jar of perfume, and as she stood behind him at his feet weeping, she began to wet his feet with her tears. Then she wiped them with her hair, kissed them and poured perfume on them."

What a compromising position to be in! Jesus is visiting the local religious leader when a woman who was a known prostitute comes in and begins to wash his feet with tears and perfume. Would you have let such a scene go on? Well, Jesus did. In fact, when the Pharisee commented on how inappropriate the whole situation was, Jesus used his discomfort as an opportunity to teach on forgiveness and love.

Jesus' primary concern was not what other people thought of him. What mattered to him was accepting people and allowing them to be exactly who they were within the context of God's forgiveness. His life wasn't about asking people to change so they could be saved. It was about introducing them to a salvation and love that would result in change.

Jesus' disciples saw the way he accepted others. As a result of his example, the Apostle John would later write:

"Dear friends, let us love one another, for love comes from God. Everyone who loves has been born of God and knows God. Whoever does not love does not know God, because God is love" (1 John 4:7-8).

John saw love and acceptance in Jesus, and it changed his life forever. Your students, too, need to see Christ's love and acceptance in you. Here's a few ways you can model an attitude of acceptance in your class.

• Don't focus on your reputation. In Romans 12:16, Paul tells us, "Do not be proud, but be willing to associate with people of low position." Sometimes we make ourselves believe that we avoid interacting with "sinners" because we don't want to misrepresent Christ by appearing to condone their sinful ways. But the truth is we're often more worried about our own reputations than we are about Christ's. Jesus didn't care if people judged him for associating with sinners. All he cared about was revealing and extending God's love to people who needed it. As teachers following in his ways, we should extend the same love toward "people of low position," even when that means our own reputations will be knocked down a few notches because of it.

• Celebrate differences. Most churches quickly become havens for conformity. We dress alike, talk alike, and tend to think alike on most issues. That sense of external conformity can lead some people to believe that diverse perspectives or varying personal styles are not accepted in your church. You can model acceptance by celebrating the differences between your students and recognizing those differences as strengths.

• Share your testimony. Almost anyone who has come to Christ can remember times he or she made bad choices in life—choices that God

> *"A sportscaster can say, 'That guy is a lousy point guard,' but he can only say that because the guy is on the court. You don't take shots at other people on the sidelines—just the players who are out there doing something. So the people that actually risk—get out there—are the ones who are going to get hammered at times. And that's what Jesus did. He went out, risked, put himself out there to be criticized. And I could say that for any leader. If you go out and do something, you're going to get hammered, because you're going to be out on the court."*
>
> —Rick Lawrence

has forgiven and corrected. Rather than hide these "dark" episodes from your students, openly share them. Telling others about your failures will help people realize that God accepts them, too, no matter what they might have done in the past.

4. Jesus modeled the importance of rest. Not only did Jesus regularly go off alone to private, restful places, but he also encouraged his disciples to do the same. In Mark 6:30-32, after the disciples returned from their first "mission trip," Jesus encouraged them to take it easy for a while.

"The apostles gathered around Jesus and reported to him all they had done and taught. Then, because so many people were coming and going that they did not even have a chance to eat, he said to them, 'Come with me by yourselves to a quiet place and get some rest.' So they went away by themselves in a boat to a solitary place."

In another scene recorded in John 11, when Jesus learned that his friend Lazarus was dying, he did not respond the way most of us might. Instead of dropping everything and running to Lazarus' side, the Scripture says that "when he heard that Lazarus was sick, he stayed where he was two more days" (John 11:6). How different that is from some of us whose lives can often be described as an endless string of reactions to the crises we continually encounter.

Jesus rested in the guiding power of the Holy Spirit. He rested in the knowledge that his heavenly Father was in control, so he didn't have to be. Jesus knew how to rest, and he modeled that rest for his disciples.

How can you model "rest" for your students? Consider these simple ideas:

• Be "Christ-controlled"—not "need-controlled." Jesus didn't meet every need he encountered, nor did he base his choices solely on what people asked him to do. Instead, he followed the Holy Spirit in making his choices about where to go and who to help. Sometimes that meant helping others when he was tired. But other times it meant stealing away to rest alone with God. By following God's Spirit, you can enter into his rest (see Hebrews 4), and demonstrate true "rest" in a way that will inspire others to follow.

• Turn some of your meetings with students into "fun times." Go see a movie together, have a meal, or throw a surprise birthday party for someone in the group. Let students see that you value fun and rest as an integral part of life.

• Simplify your life. Prayerfully take stock of all that you do each week, and weed out any activities that you believe aren't part of God's will for your life now. But be warned! Some of the things God leads you to let go of might be "good" activities that you enjoy. Even so, strive to be obedient to God's will, and set an example of rest for your students.

5. Jesus modeled freedom in God. In Matthew 11:19, Jesus said, "The Son of Man came eating and drinking, and they say, 'Here is a glutton and a drunkard, a friend of tax collectors and "sinners." ' But wisdom is proved right by her actions."

C'mon, a glutton and a drunkard? Our Savior? No way! But that's what some people called him. And, most likely, the ones who called him that were religious types, who would never be caught dead at a party with "sinners" or cavorting with the locals in the rough part of town.

Jesus wasn't that way. He broke the norm for the rabbi. He enjoyed the company of common folk. He even played with children (despite his disciples' efforts to keep kids away from him). In short, he had nothing to prove to anyone, so he was free to be himself. His freedom was based not in irreverence toward God, but in reverence. Not in mockery of his authority but in the absolute security of it. And, as a result, some people labeled him a glutton and a drunkard.

There's one principle of life you can always count on: People who aren't free hate to be around people who are. In fact, they hate it so much that they will slander you, accuse you of all sorts of sin, and even threaten your life (as they did with Jesus). In fact, that's one way you can tell whether you're walking in true freedom, by noticing how "religious" people—Pharisee types—respond to you. If you find yourself accused of "wild living" when you know you're devoted to following God's will, it may actually be a positive sign that you're on the right track.

As a teacher, though, modeling freedom in Christ is especially difficult, because you have to balance your desire to demonstrate freedom for your students with the Bible's warning to do nothing to offend your brother or cause him to stumble. Even though it can be tricky, there are some easy things you can do to set an example of freedom for your students.

Teacher's Corner: Modeling Freedom for Children

As teachers, we're often tempted to project an image to children of what we think they expect a leader to be: solemn, wise, and serious. But that's not the sort of leader Jesus was or is today. And that's not the sort of leader children necessarily need to see either.

One of the most powerful ways you can model freedom for children is by being willing to play freely with them—on their own level. That doesn't mean you have to let go of control or create an atmosphere of chaos in the classroom. But it's important to realize that children can have fun and learn at the same time. In fact, that's how they're designed to learn: through *play.*

Of course, the ability to model childlike playfulness for your kids may not come to you overnight. It requires vulnerability, trust, and a wonderful absence of self-awareness. But as you allow kids to see your own childlike, fun nature, they will learn to value their own freedom and find ways to protect it from the inevitable drain of growing up.

• Spend time developing relationships with non-Christians. Christians who lose touch with the non-Christian world around them can quickly become ingrown and insulated from the real world, making them ineffective at reaching out to non-Christians and understanding their struggles. To prevent this from happening, get to know your neighbors. Join a local club or sign up for a class at the community center. Make relating to non-Christians a regular part of your life. After all, they are the people Jesus came to save.

• Explain your motives behind living the way you do. If you think it's OK to go to bars, explain to your students why you think so. If you drink, explain to your students why you do. Don't leave students in the dark about the freedoms you embrace, especially if you know other Christians might disagree with your choices.

"When I think back to the people who have really impacted me, there really hasn't been anything about what they said, but the way that they moved through life revealed something of God's character or what he desires from me. The way they responded to me was a reflex, just like I have reflexes, but their reflexes were Christlike, and that stunned me and made me very curious about them."

—Rick Lawrence

• Don't give in to the pressure of false religion. In Matthew 12:1-8, the Pharisees noticed Jesus' disciples picking grain on the Sabbath and eating it as they walked along. The Scripture says, "When the Pharisees saw this, they said to him, 'Look! Your disciples are doing what is unlawful on the Sabbath' " (Matthew 12:2). In response, Jesus didn't tell his disciples to stop, nor did he reprimand them later for picking grain in front of the Pharisees—something they surely would have known would upset such a religious crowd. Instead, he allowed his disciples to continue what they were doing while he *reprimanded the Pharisees.*

As teachers, there will also be "Pharisee types" who will challenge our freedom in Christ. But when that happens, we should stand firm, for our own sake as well as for the sake of our students. As Paul states, "It is for freedom that Christ has set us free. Stand firm, then, and do not let yourselves be burdened again by a yoke of slavery" (Galatians 5:1).

John Wesley once received a note that said: "The Lord...doesn't need your book-learning, your Greek and your Hebrew."

Wesley reacted to this attack on his freedom by writing this response: "Thank you, sir. Your letter was superfluous, however, as I already knew the Lord has no need for my 'book-learning...' I would like to say to you that the Lord does not need your ignorance either."[5]

• If your freedom causes a brother or sister to stumble, ask forgiveness and change your behavior. In Galatians 5:13, Paul offers this warning: "You, my brothers, were called to be free. But do not use your freedom to indulge the sinful nature; rather, serve one another in love." Flaunting your freedom "because you can" is not a loving choice and can quickly lead to division in the body of Christ. Your freedom in Christ must never take precedence over Jesus' mandate to love one another. Therefore, any freedom you have that injures your brother—*even if his injury is caused by his own weakness in faith*—must be stopped immediately. Remember, your goal as a teacher is to draw students into a closer relationship with God. If what you do out of freedom in Christ causes some of your students to stumble, why keep doing it? Be free, but more importantly, be loving.

Teacher's Corner:
Mentoring: Revealing Jesus to Others—
One Person at a Time

I once knew a young man who grew up in a troubled home. His father was absent most of the time, and even when he was home, his attention was given almost exclusively to the television, or the newspaper, or the pile of work in his study that never seemed to go away. And no matter what good he did—in school or athletics or hobbies—it never seemed to be good enough to warrant his father's attention or approval.

Luckily, the young man attended church regularly. When he was sixteen, an older man in the church took notice of him. He saw something special in that young man—something worth investing in. And so he invested in his life. He took the boy out for a Coke or to play video games. He listened. He prayed. And he told the boy what he saw—a special young man with a heart for God and a passion for life. That man's name was Tommy Macintosh. In the eyes of the world, he was a dwarf—not quite four feet tall. But to the young man, he was a giant. That "big" little man was able to see what the boy's parents had missed. And my life has never been the same since.

I was one of the lucky ones—those few young people in the church who get to experience what it's like to have an older man or woman be a "champion" for your life. In fact, after Tommy moved away, I was mentored by another man of God named Brad Bankhead. I would not be where I am today if it had not been for those men. I am living proof of the powerful impact a mentor can have, not just on one life, but on all the lives I have touched since I met them. You see, since my youth, I have become a mentor myself. And I can tell you without reservation that I benefit more now from mentoring than I ever did when I was younger.

Establishing a mentoring ministry in your church can seem like an organizational nightmare. But it doesn't have to be. All mentoring really involves is building relationships between older and younger people—seniors with youth, singles with families, youth with children. As a pastor or teacher, all you have to do is find ways to get people together and allow God to knit those mentoring relationships in the way he desires.

Of course, some mentoring programs are more formal, and that may be what your church body needs. If so, you'll need to establish goals and expectations, set up appropriate screening and matching programs, provide an adequate communication network, and organize activities for mentors and their protégés to do together.

Although these kinds of mentoring programs are good, they are not always essential. Mentoring can be as unstructured as a Christian mechanic tinkering on cars with the neighborhood kids. It can be short-term, such as providing tutoring during finals week. Or it can be as simple as asking a young man out for a Coke.

In his book *Mentoring*, Bobb Biehl says that to be an effective mentor, you only need to be able to ask two questions:

1. What are your priorities?

2. How can I help?[6]

Suddenly, mentoring doesn't sound so complicated, does it? And, really, it's not. But the impact it can have—on mentors and protégés alike—can change lives forever.

Where to Begin

So now that you have all these ideas, what should you do with them? How can you begin to teach by example this week? Paul outlined the answer for us in 2 Corinthians 4:1-2, 5-7.

"Therefore, since through God's mercy we have this ministry, we do not lose heart. Rather, we have renounced secret and shameful ways; we do not use deception, nor do we distort the word of God. On the contrary, by setting forth the truth plainly we commend ourselves to every man's conscience in the sight of God. For we do not preach ourselves, but Jesus Christ as Lord, and ourselves as your servants for Jesus' sake. For God, who said, 'Let light shine out of darkness,' made his light shine in our hearts to give us the light of the knowledge of the glory of God in the face of Christ. But we have this treasure in jars of clay to show that this all-surpassing power is from God and not from us."

Even though Paul is talking about the big picture of the "ministry of reconciliation" we all have as Christians, the principles he lists here can also apply to the responsibility of Christians to model God's truth by the way we live. In effect, Paul's words can become an instructional template for anyone who wants to teach by example. Let's break it down:

1. "We have renounced secret and shameful ways." We can't harbor secret sins and hope to be an effective model for Jesus. So the first step

toward preparing yourself to teach by example is to take a self-inventory, then turn away from any sin that you may be harboring in your life.

2. "We do not use deception, nor do we distort the word of God. On the contrary, by setting forth the truth plainly we commend ourselves to every man's conscience in the sight of God." In other words, don't try to hide the facts or "make yourself look good" in front of your students. Let them see the real you, warts and all. Conversely, don't try to gloss over what the Bible says about choices you've made in the past. Be honest about who you are and clear about what the Bible teaches.

3. "For we do not preach ourselves, but Jesus Christ as Lord, and ourselves as your servants for Jesus' sake." Finally, make it clear that Jesus is the One your students should follow—not you. Explain that your actions as a role model aren't designed to get people to admire you. Your only goal as a servant is to get people to follow Christ.

By following these three steps, and adopting some of the ideas suggested in this chapter, you'll be on your way toward living out the "heart" of teaching others by your example. And don't worry. It's really not as hard as you think. In fact, all the ideas we've suggested here can be summed up in one simple statement, which we'll list as Principle 8.

Principle 8
Be to them as Christ is to you.

That's the heart of modeling. We strive to reveal Christ through our lives, in the same way that Jesus revealed the Father through his. The only difference: Jesus revealed God perfectly, but we reveal Jesus through humble jars of clay.

"But we have this treasure in jars of clay to show that this all-surpassing power is from God and not from us."

—2 Corinthians 4:7

[1] Story adapted from *Illustrations Unlimited,* ed. by James S. Hewett (Wheaton, IL: Tyndale House Publishers, 1988), 313. Used by permission. All rights reserved.

[2] William Barclay, *The Mind Of Jesus* (New York, NY: Harper & Row, 1961), 172.

[3] Warren S. Benson, "Christ the Master Teacher," in *Christian Education: Foundations for the Future,* ed. by Robert E. Clark, Len Johnson, and Allyn K. Sloat (Chicago, IL: Moody Press, 1991). 98. Quoted in *Teaching as Jesus Taught,* 121.

[4] Elmer L. Towns, *Fasting for Spiritual Breakthrough* (Ventura, CA: Regal Books, 1996), 17-18.

[5] *Illustrations Unlimited,* ed. by James S. Hewett (Wheaton, IL: Tyndale House Publishers, 1988), 315. Used by permission. All rights reserved.

[6] Bobb Biehl, *Mentoring* (Nashville, TN: Broadman & Holman Publishers, 1996), 24.

Chapter 9
Your Game Plan for Teaching Like Jesus

"I tell you the truth, anyone who has faith in me
will do what I have been doing.
He will do even greater things than these,
because I am going to the Father."
—*John 14:12*

Helen Keller once wrote:

> I believe that life is given us so we may grow in love, and I believe that God is in me as the sun is in the color and fragrance of a flower—the Light in my darkness, the Voice in my silence.[1]

Probably the greatest challenge to teaching like Jesus is believing that it's possible. No matter how confident we are in our speaking ability, how firmly we believe in the Gospel, or how much we want to help people grow in faith, there's typically a part of us that resists believing that God would ever want to use us in a powerful way to impact others. Something in us says:

- I'm not good enough.
- I can't hear God.
- I'm not worth God's notice.
- I don't have anything special to offer.
- I could never live up to the standard God expects.
- I wouldn't know where to begin.

We are aware of God's great power and love in the same way Helen Keller was aware of the existence of light and sound. But like her, we often feel incapable of connecting with those distant realities in any practical way. Fortunately for Helen, she discovered that God was big enough to fill in the gaps in her human ability. He filled her life with light so dramatically that she could teach a lesson about the colors in a flower that she had never seen with her physical eyes.

God is big enough to work through our shortcomings, too. Consider these encouraging words from Paul:

"Such confidence as this is ours through Christ before God. Not that we are competent in ourselves to claim anything for ourselves, but our competence comes from God. He has made us competent as ministers of a new covenant—not of the letter, but of the Spirit; for the letter kills, but the Spirit gives life" (2 Corinthians 3:4-6).

"But God chose the foolish things of the world to shame the wise; God chose the weak things of the world to shame the strong. He chose the lowly things of this world and the despised things—and the things that are not—to nullify the things that are, so that no one may boast before him. It is because of him that you are in Christ Jesus, who has become for us wisdom from God—that is, our righteousness, holiness and redemption" (1 Corinthians 1:27-30).

So if you ever feel foolish, weak, lowly, or despised, then you're a perfect candidate for becoming a teacher like Jesus. All you have to do is say yes.

Teachers of Purpose

Once you do accept God's invitation to teach the way Jesus taught, what then? The most important adjustment you'll need to make is to realize that teaching like Jesus means that everything we do as teachers must be purposeful, practical, and based on the principles we've explored. As a teacher, Jesus never did anything without a reason. To teach like him, neither should we. Every game, every question, and every lecture or activity needs to be purposeful and focused on a goal. Since we have less time to spend with students than Jesus did with his disciples, this principle is doubly important. It's an essential paradigm shift for anyone who wants to follow in his steps.

Principle 9
Do everything with a purpose.

Waste no opportunity through unfocused busy-work, purposeless games, or useless rituals that students do just because "we've always done it that way." Instead, focus every activity, every game, and every experience on your ultimate purpose. And what is that purpose? *To draw people into personal, genuine relationships with God.*

In addition to staying focused on the goal, our teaching must be founded and constructed on the principles we've explored. To help you remember these principles and build your teaching around them, make several photocopies of the "Jesus' Teaching Principles" list on page 180, and place them where you'll see them often. For example, put one copy in your Bible, another in your daily planner, and another on the wall next to your desk. Keeping the principles in front of you will help you remember to use them as the foundation for the lessons you create.

Being purposeful and principle-centered in your teaching won't happen overnight. It will take time, focus, and an openness to risk. You may be tempted to try to incorporate all the lessons you've learned into your teaching right away. Don't. Instead, pace yourself. Give yourself (and your students!) time to adjust to new ideas and new ways of doing things. By starting small, then gradually building principle on principle, you'll still be able to totally transform your teaching within a matter of weeks. And by making changes slowly, each change will not only seem more natural, it will inspire you to keep going, perfecting each technique until the transformation is complete.

The pages that follow contain a detailed blueprint for beginning your transformation toward becoming a teacher like Jesus. Take time to go through this process carefully before making a single change. Answer the questions honestly. Then set realistic, measurable goals to help you gauge your progress. Putting forth a little effort now ensures that the changes you make later will not only be accurate, but will have a lasting impact on your students' lives.

"Suppose one of you wants to build a tower. Will he not first sit down and estimate the cost to see if he has enough money to complete it? For if he lays the foundation and is not able to finish it, everyone who sees it will ridicule him, saying, 'This fellow began to build and was not able to finish' "(Luke 14:28-30).

Eight Steps to Transform Your Teaching

Carefully work through these steps to begin the transformation

Jesus' Teaching Principles

1. *Realize that people cannot understand truth unless God enables them.*

2. *The ultimate goal of Christian teaching is to draw people into a genuine, personal relationship with God.*

3. *Believe that if they are teachable, they will learn.*

4. *Maximize your maxims.*

5. *Use lecture to reveal Jesus—not just your topic.*

6. *Teach, test, and solidify learning through real-life experiences.*

7. *To teach well, question well.*

8. *Be to them as Christ is to you.*

9. *Do everything with a purpose.*

toward teaching the way Jesus taught.

1. Know the Goal.

To be purposeful teachers, we must always keep our goal in mind. Every activity that we create—from crowdbreakers to Bible studies to real-life experiences—must be focused toward that goal.

That doesn't mean that we can't talk about any topic other than "how to have a personal, vibrant relationship with God." In fact, there are a myriad of topics that should be discussed in your classroom—from "abortion" to "relationships" to "zeal." Any topic that is of practical concern to your students should be openly addressed. But staying focused on the goal means that all the topics we cover should be framed within the context of our relationship with God. If you talk about abortion, ask students to defend their views as an expression of obedience to God. If you discuss relationships, challenge students to see their interactions with others as an extension of their relationship with God. And if you want to inspire people to be zealous, encourage them to get excited about following Jesus rather than pursuing some cause or social movement. Constantly evaluate everything you do by asking one simple question:

Will this (activity, question, experience, lecture, discussion, parable, or saying) draw people closer to Jesus?

If the answer is yes, great! You're right on track. If the answer is no, alter what you're doing—until it falls in line with the goal.

To help you keep the goal in mind in all that you do, photocopy the "Teaching Like Jesus: Know the Goal" section on page 182, and place it somewhere you will see it often. Look over the goals and objectives listed there every time you begin to design a lesson for your students. Keeping the goal in front of you all the time will keep you focused and help you "hit the target" every time you teach.

2. Know Your Students.

Jesus knew his audience and altered his approach and technique depending on the type of person or people he dealt with. He was confrontational with some and gentle with others, depending on the student. And no matter how he taught, he used examples, stories, and illustrations that were common to people's lives to help them grasp the truths he wanted to teach.

Teaching Like Jesus:
Know the Goal

The Ultimate Goal of Teaching
To draw people into a genuine, personal relationship with God.

Objectives for Disciples
1. To build relationships.
2. To train in love.
3. To train in faith and obedience.
4. To send in boldness.

Objectives for Seekers (and Disciples)
1. To encourage in faith.
2. To challenge people to think.
3. To provoke to decision.

Objective to Opponents
1. To expose hypocrisy, pride, and unbelief.

What kind of people do you have in your group? Are there any engineers, musicians, sports enthusiasts, teachers? By knowing just a little about your students, you can shape your lesson examples and illustrations around elements that are common to their lives.

To help you learn more about your students and teach them more effectively, have them complete the "Getting to Know You Better Questionnaire" on page 184. Keep the information on file, and update it often as a way to glean ideas for how you can best present the truths you want to teach.

Teacher's Corner: If You Teach Young Children...

If you teach a class of younger children, you might suggest that parents complete the questionnaire for their kids. You may need to modify a few of the questions depending on the age group you teach.

---

3. Know Yourself.

Every teacher has inherent strengths and weaknesses. You may be great at leading fun activities but feel awkward when forced to tell a serious story. You probably already have a good idea of which aspects of teaching you're best at and which areas could use work. But teaching like Jesus requires more than just knowing where your strengths and weaknesses lie as a teacher. You also need to know the strengths and weaknesses of your own relationship with God. That's because teaching like Jesus is essentially "incarnational" teaching. The goal of teaching like Jesus isn't simply to copycat his techniques, but rather to learn how to let the Holy Spirit teach through you, using the same methods that Jesus used (see 1 Corinthians 2:12-13). That means that if any area of your personal relationship with God is weak or undeveloped, it will show up in your teaching and make you less effective.

As you begin the journey toward teaching like Jesus, take stock of your personal relationship with God. Focus on those areas that seem weak or inconsistent. For example, you may excel at giving to people in need but fall short when it comes to praying consistently for the people closest to you.

What specific aspects of your relationship with God are strong? Which areas need work? To help you begin to answer these questions, complete the "Where I Stand Self-Evaluation" on pages 185-186. Then begin to focus your personal time with God on those areas that need greater attention.

Getting to Know You Better
Questionnaire

1. What's your full name?

2. When and where were you born?

3. Who else is in your family?

4. What are some of your favorite hobbies or interests?

5. What was your favorite thing to do as a child?

6. What's one fact about you that few people know?

7. What's one dream you'd like to accomplish in your lifetime?

8. What do you think is the most important issue facing the world today?

9. What's one positive thing you'd like to see happen in your life this year?

10. How would you describe your personality to someone who doesn't know you?

Where I Stand
Self-Evaluation[2]

Answer "yes" or "no" to each question below. Then focus your personal time with God on developing those areas that seem weak.

QUESTIONS   **YES/NO**

The Bible

Do I love to read and study God's Word?

Do I strive to consistently apply the Bible to my life?

Sin and Forgiveness

Am I quick to confess my sins to God?

Do I typically ask for forgiveness when I wrong someone?

Is my conscience clear with everyone I know?

Love

Do I love what God loves and hate what God hates?

Do I consistently show love to others in what I say and do?

Obedience

Does my schedule reveal that God is first in my life?

Is my life characterized by genuine sacrifice for Jesus?

Am I keeping in step with the Spirit?

Personal Character

Am I more concerned about what God thinks of my life than about what people think?

Am I willing to give up sin for God?

Is my life free of moral impurity?

Sharing Faith

Do I genuinely care about people who don't know Christ?

Do I consistently share my faith with non-Christians—through my words and actions?

Prayer

Do I consistently pray for the needs of others?

Is worship an integral part of my prayer life?

Relationships

Do I make it my ambition to "fervently love" my family and friends?

Are all of my relationships healthy and glorifying to God?

4. Evaluate Your Teaching Style.

You know the goal. You understand your students. And you've begun to strengthen your personal relationship with God. Now you're ready to explore where you're going *as a teacher*. But to know where you're going, you first have to know where you are. That means you need to evaluate your present teaching style before you can set realistic goals toward teaching more like Jesus.

Pull out your notes from the last four lessons you taught. (If you don't keep your notes, just do this exercise from memory.) Think through all the activities you did, questions you asked, and stories you told in those four lessons. Then fill in the following chart.

"One thing seems clear to me. Jesus didn't really deal with excuses that much. He didn't make way for anyone's excuse about why they wouldn't go or shouldn't go or couldn't follow. I can't remember a time when he asked somebody to follow, they gave a reason why they couldn't, and he accepted it."

—Rick Lawrence

My Last Four Lessons

Total number...		Total amount of time spent on this technique (in all four lessons combined)	Average amount of time spent on this technique (Total time÷4)
...of lectures:			
...of discussions:			
...of parables:			
...of sayings or maxims:			
...of learning experiences:			
...of questions:			
...of "other" (please specify):			

Now consider how your teaching might change if you always taught the way Jesus taught in your classroom. In the next chart, imagine how you'd spend your time (in a one-hour lesson) if you used only Jesus' techniques when you taught. Then fill in the blanks accordingly.

Please note: The point here is not to say that we must include each of Jesus' techniques in every lesson we teach. Like Jesus, sometimes we might focus exclusively on parables, while other times we might lead students through a lengthy real-life experience. Instead, think of the chart as a way of describing the average amount of time you'd spend on each of Jesus' techniques if you consistently taught the way he did.

My Ideal Jesus-Style Lesson

Total number...		Average amount of time I wish I spent using this technique
...of lectures:		
...of discussions:		
...of parables:		
...of sayings or maxims:		
...of learning experiences:		
...of questions:		

Now combine the results of the last two charts in the space on the next page.

My Teaching Evaluation Results

	Average amount of time I spend...	Average amount of time I wish I spent...	I should: 1. Do more of this. 2. Do less of this. 3. Keep things as they are.
...giving lectures:			
...leading discussions:			
...using parables:			
...teaching sayings or maxims:			
...guiding students through learning experiences:			
...asking questions:			

Teacher's Corner: Use of Questions

Remember that leading discussions and asking questions aren't always the same thing. Many questions Jesus asked were never intended to spark open discussion, while many of the discussions he led were actually started by allowing students to ask the questions!

5. Set Long-Term and Short-Term Goals.

Now that you've evaluated where you are, you're ready to set a course toward where you want to go. Based on what you wrote in the "My Teaching Evaluation Results" box, you can now set some long-term goals for your teaching style by filling in the following chart. Make sure your goals are realistic and measurable. For example, instead of writing "Use more parables" (which isn't very measurable), choose something more specific, such as "I will include at least one parable per month in my lessons." Think carefully about each area before constructing your goal. These will become guideposts to direct you as you move through the next several weeks.

"You can't make general-izations based on individual episodes of how Jesus taught and say, 'That's the way to teach.' I think part of the message we're getting is that he taught different ways for different individuals. Some people needed to be confronted with something that was uncomfortable; other people 'got it' without that."

—Thom Schultz

Here are my long-term goals...

...for using lecture as a teaching tool:

...for using discussion as a teaching tool:

...for using parables as a teaching tool:

...for using maxims and sayings as a teaching tool:

...for using real-life experiences as a teaching tool:

...for using questions as a teaching tool:

...for using modeling as a teaching tool:

Teacher's Corner:
Setting Goals for Modeling Your Faith

Modeling is one of the hardest aspects of teaching to measure or set goals for. After all, modeling is a behind-the-scenes, full-time affair. It wouldn't do much good to set a goal such as, "I will model my faith for students on a regular basis," because such a goal isn't really measurable. How will you tell if you've succeeded?

To make the goal more measurable, make it more specific. For example, "I will model intimacy with God by praying with students during every lesson." Or you could make it even more challenging by saying, "I will model my faith in front of my students in such a way that they openly describe me as one who walks intimately with God, prays often, and is free from worry."

Now you're ready to set your short-term goals. Remember to keep your long-term goals in mind as you create your short-term goals. These goals will chart a realistic, measurable course from where you are to where you want to be. The following chart is set up to allow you twelve weeks to successfully reach your long-term goals. That may seem like a long time, but you'll be making changes all along the way, so you won't be bored. And you'll give yourself plenty of time to incorporate each new change before moving on to the next one.

I suggest you set your goals by addressing one new aspect of teaching every two weeks. Then as each short-term goal is achieved, move on to the next area of teaching you want to focus on. By the end of the twelfth week, you should have achieved each of your long-term goals.

You may tackle the various techniques in any order you wish. I've listed each on the chart below for your convenience.

"Do we have an expectation of God's power showing up in what we intend to teach? Do we expect that? Somewhere along the line, in what we're directing these kids to do, we should believe that God's power will become evident."

—Rick Lawrence

Teaching areas to focus on:

Lecture	Experiences
Discussions	Questions
Parables and Sayings	Modeling

	Area to focus on	**Goals**
Week 1		
Week 3		
Week 5		
Week 7		
Week 9		
Week 11		

Transfer your short-term goals to your calendar or daily planner so that you'll be reminded of what you need to focus on as you prepare your lesson for that week.

6. Be Accountable.

You're about to undertake a significant transformation in your teaching style. You'll face many challenges along the way—some you will expect, while others may catch you completely unaware. You'll need perseverance to see these changes through to the end. You'll need encouragement along the way. You'll need people you can talk to and pray with. And you'll need people who will talk honestly with you about what you're doing and offer sound advice when needed. In short, you'll need a support group.

Teaching like Jesus involves risk. Some people will resist the changes you want to make. Some will misunderstand your motives. And some will criticize you openly. You need a group of people around you who can help you sift through your questions and concerns so that your teaching stays biblical—and your heart stays intact.

Think about two or three people you know whom you respect and trust. Ask them over for dinner, and explain what you're trying to do. Show them your goals, and ask them if they'd be willing to hold you accountable to follow through on the changes you want to make. Share with them your concerns. Ask them to pray for you. And be willing to listen humbly to their suggestions as you work toward achieving your long-term goals.

Here are a few tips to help you decide who you should ask to be a part of your support group:

• Ask people who know you well and believe in you.

• If possible, ask people whose strengths are different from yours. (They can help give a more well-rounded perspective on your teaching goals.)

• Ask the leaders in your church (your pastor or CE director). Even if they can't commit to be a part of your group, be sure to keep them informed about everything you're trying to do.

• If you teach youth or adults, consider including one or more of your students in your support group.

Once your support group is in place, talk with them regularly about how you're doing, and discuss any concerns that come up as a result of the changes you're making.

7. Start Now.

Procrastination is one of the greatest obstacles to positive change. So once you've outlined your goals, and your support group is in place, begin pursuing your goals right away. Don't fall into the trap of finding convenient excuses to "wait until next week" to start making changes. Begin right now, starting with the next lesson you teach. Use the "Teaching Like Jesus Lesson Planner" (pp. 194-197) to help you organize your next lesson around the goals you've set. And feel free to photocopy the planner so you can use it for future lessons you create.

"I think he [Jesus] had done a lot of things here and there to reveal to them who he was. But I don't think they had yet grasped the concept that the same power was available to them. What he was challenging them to think about was the power that was available to them through him."

—Paul Woods

8. Evaluate the Effect.

Once you've implemented the changes in your teaching, you'll need to measure your success—not only in how effectively you meet your short- and long-term goals, but also in how your students respond. If you're applying these principles effectively, you should begin to see growth in your students—particularly those whose hearts are sincere and genuinely interested in learning.

There are several ways to get feedback from students to help you measure the impact of your teaching on their lives. Here are several quick tips you can use right away:

• Guide students through real-life purposeful experiences. As we've discovered, Jesus sometimes measured learning by placing his disciples in situations where they were forced to apply the lessons he taught. You can do the same thing by guiding your students through purposeful experiences that you plan for them. For more information on this kind of "real world" experience, review pages 124 to 133.

• Use an evaluation card. Use statements like these: "One thing I've learned recently through this class is..." or "One thing that still confuses me is..." Then use the information to help you measure what students are really learning and how you can improve.

Teaching Like Jesus
Lesson Planner

Date:

Lesson Topic:

Scripture Basis:

Point of the Lesson:

Designing the Lesson

Sayings and Maxims

- Is there a Bible verse that states the point effectively on its own? (For example, "Do unto others as you would have them do unto you.")

- Is there a quote or famous saying that effectively states the point?

- Is there a creative way you can phrase the point of the lesson as a saying or maxim?

Experiences

- If your students could learn the point through some personal, real-life experience, what might that experience be?

- How might you reproduce an experience like that in the classroom? in a field trip; service project; or other planned, purposeful event?

Parables

- What are some stories that could illustrate or teach the point of the lesson?

Questions

- What questions do you want students to explore in this lesson?

- What sorts of questions could you ask for each of the categories below?

Conversation-starters (such as "How was your week?")

Topic-launchers (such as "How can we honor our parents?")

Fact-finders (such as "What does God's Word say about honoring parents?")

Thought-provokers (such as "What makes you feel 'honored' by others?" "How can you apply that to 'honoring' your parents?")

Sin-confronters (such as "How can you claim to love your parents if you will not honor them in daily life?")

Faith-encouragers (such as "Don't you believe that God will bless you for honoring your parents?")

Lecture

- What facts or insights do I want to convey about the topic?

- What do I want students to learn about me based on this topic?

- How can I effectively convey that information through a lecture?

Discussion

- What are issues for discussion that the students might bring up?

- How can I help facilitate discussion on those issues to maximize learning?

Modeling

- How can I model this lesson through the way that I live?

Now, based on the ideas you've generated, create an outline of the lesson you'd like to teach. Use as many (or as few) of the spaces provided to outline your lesson, depending on the number of activities you want to include. Be sure to include a list of needed supplies, and write out any key questions you want to ask throughout the meeting.

Date of Lesson:

Lesson Point:

Bible Basis:

Activities	Supplies
Activity 1	
Activity 2	
Activity 3	
Activity 4	
Activity 5	
Activity 6	

• Set up a suggestion box. Encourage students to write out suggestions, comments, or questions about your teaching whenever they wish. Then check the box frequently and address any questions or concerns students might have.

• Pay attention to students' prayer requests. When you pray together, take note of what students ask the group to pray about. You'd be surprised how much you can discover about what students are learning just by listening to their prayers.

• Ask questions. Create an open atmosphere in your classroom that invites students to talk about their lives, the lessons they're learning, or any problems they may be having with the teaching. Don't feel frustrated or defensive if students don't seem to be grasping what you're trying to teach. Instead, use their comments to help you discover which techniques work best with your class.

> *"You'll know you've understood when you see your behavior changing."*
>
> —Rick Lawrence

A Teacher Like Jesus

I once read a legend about a missionary teacher who was lost at sea, and, by chance, washed up on the shore near a remote island village. Nearly dead from starvation and exposure to the sun, the man lay on the beach for over a day before the local villagers found him. The villagers took in the stranger and nursed him back to health. Once he recovered, the teacher decided to stay in the village for awhile and do what he could to help the people there. He ended up living with them for more than a year. During that time, he had great trouble learning the language because it was so different from his own. But when someone got sick, he cared for them, sometimes staying up late into the night. When the people were hungry, he showed them new ways to raise crops so they could have more food. When people were lonely, he'd stay with them, joking around or playing a game until they felt better. And when someone was treated unfairly, he would intervene, demonstrating to people the need to show love and forgiveness.

After a year or so had passed, another group of missionaries came to the village. They knew the language and began to tell people about Jesus, and how much he loved them. As they described Jesus, the villagers interrupted and said, "We already know this Jesus. He's been living in the village for over a year. Come, we'll introduce you to him." The missionaries were led to a hut and immediately recognized the man as a missionary friend who they believed had been lost at sea.[3]

To teach as Jesus taught, it's good—and important—to study his methods, learn his techniques, and incorporate them into our own teaching. But even copying every aspect of his teaching to the letter will not guarantee that we will truly become "teachers like Jesus." Ultimately, it's not the methodology that will change people's lives. It's Jesus himself, expressing his life through us in a way that leads other people to see him and want to follow him.

Another teacher, Joani Schultz, once told me:

> It's only because of the connection with Christ that I think the whole idea of teaching as Jesus taught is possible. When I think about me as a teacher, the first thing I think of is all the things I can't do. But if I open myself to say, "God, it's you doing it. If you're going to use me, it's you," then that opens the door to tremendous possibilities.

It is my prayer that we all, as Christian teachers, would open the door to tremendous possibilities—by believing in Jesus' powerful ability to use us to teach our students about him—one lesson at a time. After all, he is the ultimate point of all our teaching.

"We proclaim him, admonishing and teaching everyone
with all wisdom, so that we may present everyone
perfect in Christ. To this end I labor,
struggling with all his energy,
which so powerfully works in me."

—Colossians 1:28-29

[1] *Illustrations Unlimited,* ed. by James S. Hewett (Wheaton, IL: Tyndale House Publishers, 1988), 189. Used by permission. All rights reserved.

[2] Some of the questions in this evaluation are adapted from "Preparation for Personal Revival" in *Generation* (Stafford, TX: Mars Hill Productions, 1997), 12-14.

[3] Adapted from a story in *Illustrations Unlimited,* ed. by James S. Hewett, 361-362. Used by permission. All rights reserved.

Scripture Index

OLD TESTAMENT

Genesis 22:1-13 ..116

32:22-32 116

Exodus 3:1-6 116

Leviticus 17:10-11 ..18

Joshua 6:1-27......116

2 Samuel

12:12-20 116

Proverbs 3:34........48

11:25 33

Jonah 2:1-10.......116

NEW TESTAMENT

Matthew

Matthew 4:1-11 60

4:18-22 39

4:23-25 59

5:1-2 91

5:2–7:27 92

5:13 .... 72, 151

5:14 .... 71, 72

5:14-15 77

5:16 60

5:22 28

5:28 28

5:29 71

5:32 28

5:34 28

5:39 28

5:44 28

5:46 136

5:46-47 151

5:48 6

6:14 87

6:19-20 70

6:21 72

6:22 72

Matthew 6:24 72

6:25 ..... 149, 151

6:26 151

6:27 ..... 136, 151

6:30 151

7:2 72

7:3 .... 137, 142

7:3-4 151

7:6 84

7:9-10 151

7:16 152

7:18 72

7:24-27 77

7:28 98

7:28-29 .... 25, 99

8:1-4 52

8:22 75

8:23-27 34

8:26 .. 137, 149, 152

9:1-8 120

9:4 .. 137, 144, 152

9:5 152

9:15 152

9:16 77

9:17 77

9:28 152

9:35 39

10:5-42 92

10:24 72

10:26 81

10:29 152

10:39 ...... 39, 71, 72, 81

11:7-9 152

11:7-19 92

11:16 152

11:19 .. 35, 72, 170

Matthew 11:20-24 .... 66, 92

11:28-29 38

12:1-8 .... 39, 172

12:2 172

12:3 152

12:25 72

12:25-45 92

12:26-27 152

12:29 152

12:33 72

12:34 .. 72, 144, 152

12:37 39

12:48 152

13:3-8 77

13:10-13 .... 69, 74, 84

13:10-17 150

13:11 84

13:16 69

13:18-23 77

13:24-30 77

13:24-43 39

13:31-32 77

13:33 77

13:36-43 77

13:44 .... 77, 80

13:45-46 77

13:47-50 77

13:51 152

13:52 77

13:54 39

14:13-14 165

14:14 59

14:22-33 .. 22, 119

14:23 163

14:28-33 52

Matthew 14:30-31 145
14:31 ... 149, 152
15:1-20 93
15:3 .... 137, 144, 152
15:6-7 22
15:14 73
15:16-17 152
15:30 59
15:34 ... 139, 152
16:6 71
16:8 152
16:9 152
16:13 ... 145, 153
16:13-20 93
16:15 ... 145, 153
16:17 48
16:24-28 92
16:25 72
16:26 .... 142, 149, 153
17:17 153
17:24-27 93
18:2-4 111
18:3-11 92
18:8 22
18:12 153
18:12-14 77
18:15-20 92
18:23-34 .. 53, 77
18:23-35 87
19:3-9 39
19:3-12 93
19:16-30 93
19:17 153
19:24 71

Matthew 19:30 ... 73, 75
20:1-16 77
20:16 81
20:21 153
20:22 153
20:23-28 93
20:26-27 73
20:32 153
21:21-22 94
21:23-27 .. 94, 143
21:25 153
21:28-32 77
21:33-44 77
21:45-46 84
22:2-14 77
22:14 73
22:15-22 94
22:18 ... 144, 153
22:20 153
22:23-33 94
22:34-40 94
22:37-39 54
22:41-46 .. 94, 136
22:42 ... 145, 153
23:1-39 92
23:8 38
23:12 73
23:17 153
23:33 153
24:2 153
24:4-44 92
24:28 71
24:32-33 77
24:45-51 77
25:1-13 77
25:14-30 .. 77, 81

Matthew 25:29 82
25:31-46 77
26:10 153
26:31 47
26:36-41 164
26:40 153
26:52 73
28:18-20 .... 9, 16

Mark
Mark 1:35 163
2:8 152
2:9 152
2:18-22 94
2:19 152
2:21 77
2:22 77
2:23-28 94
2:25 152
3:4 153
3:10 59
3:20-35 .... 23, 94
3:23 153
3:23-29 92
3:25 72
3:33 152
4:1-20 62
4:3-8 77
4:14-20 77
4:21-22 77
4:24 72
4:26-29 77
4:30 139
4:30-32 .... 71, 77
4:35-41 .. 11, 120
4:40 ..... 152, 153
5:9 .... 139, 153

Mark 5:25-34 52
    5:30 ..... 139, 153
    6:7-13 11
    6:30-32 169
    6:48-50 120
    7:1-13 30
    7:1-23 93
    7:5-15 103
    7:9-15 108
    7:6-7 39
    7:6-8 31
    7:18 152
    8:5 152
    8:12 153
    8:17 152
    8:17-18 154
    8:27 153
    8:29 153
    8:34-38 92
    8:35 72
    8:36 153
    8:37 153
    9:14-29 120
    9:16 ..... 139, 154
    9:19 153
    9:33 154
    9:50 151
    10:2-12 93
    10:3 154
    10:17-21 52
    10:17-22 66
    10:17-31 93
    10:18 153
    10:25 73
    10:31 73
    10:36 153
    10:38 153

Mark 10:39-45 93
    10:43-44 73
    10:51 153
    11:17 22
    11:20-26 94
    11:27-33 94
    11:30 153
    12:1-11 77
    12:10-11 39
    12:13-17 94
    12:15 153
    12:16 153
    12:18-27 94
    12:28-33 39
    12:28-34 94
    12:35-37 94
    12:38-40 92
    13:2 153
    13:28-29 77
    13:35-37 77
    14:6 153
    14:37 153
    17:40-41 52
    17:47 52

Luke
Luke 4:15 39
    4:31-32 99
    5:15-16 163
    5:22 152
    5:23 152
    5:33-35 94
    5:34 152
    5:36 77
    5:37-38 77
    6:1-5 94
    6:3 152

Luke 6:6 39
    6:9 153
    6:12 163
    6:20-49 92
    6:32 151
    6:33 154
    6:34 154
    6:38 72
    6:39 73
    6:40 72
    6:41-42 151
    6:43 .... 72, 73
    6:44 72
    6:45 72
    6:46 154
    6:47-49 77
    7:24-26 152
    7:24-35 92
    7:31 152
    7:36-50 120
    7:37-38 167
    7:41-43 77
    7:44 154
    8:5-8 77
    8:11-15 77
    8:16-17 77
    8:25 153
    8:30 153
    8:45 153
    9:1-6 ...... 57, 125
    9:3-5 92
    9:10-17 11
    9:18 153
    9:18-27 93
    9:20 153
    9:23-27 92
    9:23-24 158

Luke 9:24 72
9:25 153
9:41 153
10:1-12 125
10:2-24 93
10:16-20 125
10:26 154
10:30-37 77
10:38-42 120
11:1 163
11:2-13 93
11:5-8 78
11:11 151
11:17 72
11:17-36 92
11:18-19 152
11:29-32 66
11:33 77
11:34 72
11:37-52 93
11:37–12:3 66
11:40 154
12:1-12 93
12:16-21 78
12:22-34 93
12:25 142
12:25-26 154
12:34 72
12:35-40 77
12:42-48 .. 56, 77
12:49-53 93
12:54-59 93
12:56 154
12:57 154
13:6-9 78
13:17 53
13:18 139

Luke 13:18-19 77
13:20 139
13:20-21 77
13:22-30 93
14:7-14 78
14:11 73
14:16-24 .. 39, 78
14:28-30 .. 78, 179
14:31-32 78
14:34 151
15:4-7 77
15:8-10 78
15:11-32 .. 53, 78
16:1-8 78
16:15 81
16:19-31 78
17:1-6 93
17:7-10 78
17:8 49
17:17-18 154
17:20-37 93
17:33 72
18:2-8 78
18:7 154
18:8 154
18:10-14 78
18:14 73
18:17 22
18:18-30 93
18:19 153
18:41 153
19:1-9 52
19:1-10 167
19:7 167
19:11-27 109
19:12-27 77
20:1-8 94

Luke 20:4 153
20:9-18 77
20:20-26 94
20:24 153
20:27-38 94
20:41-44 94
20:45-47 92
21:29-31 77
22:24-30 93
22:26 73
22:35 ... 140, 154
22:44 46
22:48 137,
144, 154
23:31 154
24:13-35 52
24:17 ... 138, 154
24:38 154

John
John 1:14 102
1:35-51 39
1:38 138
2:13-22 128
3:1-12 52
3:1-21 ..... 63, 94,
150
3:3 .... 64, 71
3:8 71
3:10 155
3:12 .... 64, 155
3:16 64
3:21 64
4:1-30 52
4:7 .... 138, 155
4:31-38 93
4:32-35 165

John 5:1-18.......... 52
  5:6 155
  5:19 116
  5:19-47 93
  5:44 155
  6:5 .... 144, 155
  6:6 145
  6:25-59 94
  6:44-45 18
  6:44-59 17
  6:56 75
  6:60-69 20
  6:61 155
  7:14-24 .... 28, 94
  7:16-17 116
  7:18 50
  7:19 ..... 144, 155
  8:1-11 ...... 52, 53
  8:10 ..... 140, 155
  8:12-30 94
  8:12-19, 21-30 ....
               100
  8:31-58 94
  8:44 22
  8:46 ..... 149, 155
  8:50 50
  9:35 155
  10:1-18 93
  10:22-38 94
  10:32 155
  11 22
  11:1-44 120
  11:6 169
  11:17-44 53
  11:26 155
  11:39-40 145
  11:40 155

John 12:23-26...... 93
  12:25 72
  12:49 49
  13:1-9 11
  13:1-17 ... 33, 37,
               108
  13:3-7 114
  13:3-17 128
  13:7 131
  13:12 155
  13:15-16 161
  13:16 72
  13:17 130
  13:31–14:31... 94
  13:33-35 53
  13:38 155
  14 104
  14:6 ..... 102, 157
  14:8-10 157
  14:9 155
  14:12 177
  14:15 56
  14:16 117
  14:26 ..... 13, 117
  15:1–16:16......93
  15:5 39
  15:14 37
  15:16 37
  15:20 .... 40, 72
  16:13 13
  16:19-33 94
  17:1-8 47
  17:3-4 42
  17:6 .... 42, 48
  17:8 42
  17:9-11 53
  17:20-23 45

John 18:11......... 155
  18:23 155
  18:34 155
  19:28-30 53
  20:15 155
  20:19-29 22
  20:30-31 59
  21:5 ..... 138, 155
  21:15 155
  21:15-19 135
  21:22 155

Acts
Acts 9:1-16.......... 66
  22:3 51

Romans
Romans 8:9........ 117
  12:16 168

1 Corinthians
1 Corinthians
  1:26-29 162
  1:26–2:5......... 29
  1:27-30 178
  1:31 162
  2:10 5
  2:12-13 .. 13, 183
  2:14 19
  2:16 13
  6:11 64
  9:19 60
  11:1 160

2 Corinthians
2 Corinthians
  3:4-6 178

2 Corinthians

4:1-2 174

4:5-7 174

4:6-7 10

4:7 ....161, 175

10:5 16

Galatians

Galatians 1:24 ... 162

2:20 .... 10, 102

5:1 172

5:13 172

Ephesians

Ephesians

3:16-17 10

Philippians

Philippians

2:1-2 46

2:5-7 38

Colossians

Colossians 1:17 8

1:25-27 10

1:28-29 199

4:5-6 60

1 Timothy

1 Timothy 2:4 .. 11, 15

4:12 160

II Thessalonians

2 Thessalonians

2:13-14........... 37

Titus

Titus 2:7-8 161

Hebrews

Hebrews 1:3 160

James

James 2:14-17 56

3:1 56

1 Peter

1 Peter 1:13-16 .. 166

5:2-3 161

1 John

1 John 2:6........ 6, 10

4:7-8 168

Group Publishing, Inc.
Attention: Product Development
P.O. Box 481
Loveland, CO 80539
Fax: (970) 669-1994

Evaluation for *EXTRAORDINARY RESULTS FROM ORDINARY TEACHERS*

Please help Group Publishing, Inc., continue to provide innovative and useful resources for ministry. Please take a moment to fill out this evaluation and mail or fax it to us. Thanks!

● ● ●

1. As a whole, this book has been (circle one)

not very helpful   very helpful

1   2   3   4   5   6   7   8   9   10

2. The best things about this book:

3. Ways this book could be improved:

4. Things I will change because of this book:

5. Other books I'd like to see Group publish in the future:

6. Would you be interested in field-testing future Group products and giving us your feedback? If so, please fill in the information below:

Name _____

Street Address _____

City _____

State _____

Zip _____

Phone Number _____

Date _____

Exciting Resources for Your Adult Ministry

Sermon-Booster Dramas
LINCOLN CHRISTIAN COLLEGE AND SEMINARY
Tim Kurth

Now you can deliver powerful messages in fresh, new ways. Set up your message with memorable, easy-to-produce dramas—each just 3 minutes or less! These 25 low-prep dramas hit hot topics ranging from burnout...ethics...parenting...stress...to work...career issues and more! Your listeners will be on the edge of their seats!

ISBN 0-7644-2016-X

Fun Friend-Making Activities for Adult Groups
Karen Dockrey

More than 50 relational programming ideas help even shy adults talk with others at church! You'll find low-risk Icebreakers to get adults introduced and talking...Camaraderie-Builders that help adults connect and start talking about what's really happening in their lives...and Friend-Makers to cement friendships with authentic sharing and accountability.

ISBN 0-7644-2011-9

Bore No More (For Every Pastor, Speaker, Teacher)
Mike & Amy Nappa

This is a must-have for pastors, college/career speakers, and others who address groups! Because rather than just provide illustrations to entertain audiences, the authors show readers how to involve audiences in the learning process. The 70 sermon ideas presented are based on New Testament passages, but the principles apply to all passages.

ISBN 1-55945-266-8

Young Adult Faith-Launchers

These 18 in-depth Bible studies are perfect for young adults who want to strengthen their faith and deepen their relationships. They will explore real-world issues...ask the tough questions...and along the way turn casual relationships into supportive, caring friendships. Quick prep and high involvement make these the ideal studies for peer-led Bible studies, small groups, and classes.

ISBN 0-7644-2037-2

Order today from your local Christian bookstore, or write:
... 3 4711 00148 9493 ...land, CO 80539.